A TRACT ON MONETARY REFORM

The Collected Writings of John Maynard Keynes

THE COLLECTED WRITINGS OF
JOHN MAYNARD KEYNES

VOLUME IV

A TRACT
ON
MONETARY REFORM

MACMILLAN
ST MARTIN'S PRESS
FOR THE
ROYAL ECONOMIC SOCIETY

First edition 1923
Reprinted 1924, 1929, 1932
This edition 1971

Published by
THE MACMILLAN PRESS LTD
London and Basingstoke
Associated companies in New York Toronto
Dublin Melbourne Johannesburg and Madras

SBN 333 10722 5

Library of Congress catalog card no. 76-133449

Printed in Great Britain
at the University Printing House, Cambridge
(Brooke Crutchley, University Printer)

CONTENTS

GENERAL INTRODUCTION

This new standard edition of *The Collected Writings of John Maynard Keynes* forms the memorial to him of the Royal Economic Society. He devoted a very large share of his busy life to the Society. In 1911, at the age of twenty-eight, he became editor of the *Economic Journal* in succession to Edgeworth; two years later he was made secretary as well. He held these offices without intermittence until almost the end of his life. Edgeworth, it is true, returned to help him with the editorship from 1919 to 1925; Macgregor took Edgeworth's place until 1934, when Austin Robinson succeeded him and continued to assist Keynes down to 1945. But through all these years Keynes himself carried the major responsibility and made the principal decisions about the articles that were to appear in the *Economic Journal*, without any break save for one or two issues when he was seriously ill in 1937. It was only a few months before his death at Easter 1946 that he was elected president and handed over his editorship to Roy Harrod and the secretaryship to Austin Robinson.

In his dual capacity of editor and secretary Keynes played a major part in framing the policies of the Royal Economic Society. It was very largely due to him that some of the major publishing activities of the Society—Sraffa's edition of Ricardo, Stark's edition of the economic writings of Bentham, and Guillebaud's edition of Marshall, as well as a number of earlier publications in the 1930s—were initiated.

When Keynes died in 1946 it was natural that the Royal Economic Society should wish to commemorate him. It was perhaps equally natural that the Society chose to commemorate him by producing an edition of his collected works. Keynes himself had always taken a joy in fine printing, and the Society, with the help of Messrs Macmillan as publishers and the Cambridge University Press as printers, has been anxious to give

Keynes's writings a permanent form that is wholly worthy of him.

The present edition will publish as much as is possible of his work in the field of economics. It will not include any private and personal correspondence or publish letters in the possession of his family. The edition is concerned, that is to say, with Keynes as an economist.

Keynes's writings fall into five broad categories. First there are the books which he wrote and published as books. Second there are collections of articles and pamphlets which he himself made during his lifetime (*Essays in Persuasion* and *Essays in Biography*). Third, there is a very considerable volume of published but uncollected writings—articles written for newspapers, letters to newspapers, articles in journals that have not been included in his two volumes of collections, and various pamphlets. Fourth, there are a few hitherto unpublished writings. Fifth, there is correspondence with economists and concerned with economics of public affairs.

This series will attempt to publish a complete record of Keynes's serious writing as an economist. It is the intention to publish almost completely the whole of the first four categories listed above. The only exceptions are a few syndicated articles where Keynes wrote almost the same material for publication in different newspapers or in different countries, with minor and unimportant variations. In these cases, this series will publish one only of the variations, choosing the most interesting.

The publication of Keynes's economic correspondence must inevitably be selective. In the day of the typewriter and the filing cabinet and particularly in the case of so active and busy a man, to publish every scrap of paper that he may have dictated about some unimportant or ephemeral matter is impossible. We are aiming to collect and publish as much as possible, however, of the correspondence in which Keynes developed his own ideas in argument with his fellow economists, as well as the more significant correspondence at times when Keynes was in the middle of public affairs.

Apart from his published books, the main sources available to those preparing this series have been two. First, Keynes in his will made Richard Kahn his executor and responsible for his economic papers. They have been placed in the Marshall Library of the University of Cambridge and have been available for this edition. Until 1914 Keynes did not have a secretary and his earliest papers are in the main limited to drafts of important letters that he made in his own handwriting and retained. At that stage most of the correspondence that we possess is represented by what he received rather than by what he wrote. During the war years of 1914–18 Keynes was serving in the Treasury. With the recent opening of Public Records under a thirty year rule, many of the papers that he wrote then and in later years have become available. From 1919 onwards, throughout the rest of his life, Keynes had the help of a secretary—for many years Mrs Stevens. Thus for the last twenty-five years of his working life we have in most cases the carbon copies of his own letters as well as the originals of the letters that he received.

There were, of course, occasions during this period on which Keynes wrote himself in his own handwriting. In some of these cases, with the help of his correspondents, we have been able to collect the whole of both sides of some important interchange and we have been anxious, in justice to both correspondents, to see that both sides of the correspondence are published in full.

The second main source of information has been a group of scrapbooks kept over a very long period of years by Keynes's mother, Florence Keynes, wife of Neville Keynes. From 1919 onwards these scrapbooks contain almost the whole of Maynard Keynes's more ephemeral writing, his letters to newspapers and a great deal of material which enables one to see not only what he wrote, but the reaction of others to his writing. Without these very carefully kept scrapbooks the task of the editor or biographer of Keynes would have been immensely more difficult.

The plan of the edition, as at present intended, is this. It will total twenty-four volumes. Of these, the first eight will be Keynes's published books from *Indian Currency and Finance*, in 1913, to the *General Theory* in 1936, with the addition of his *Treatise on Probability*. There will next follow, as vols. IX and X, *Essays in Persuasion* and *Essays in Biography*, representing Keynes's own collections of articles. *Essays in Persuasion* will differ from the original printing in two respects; it will contain the full texts of the articles or pamphlets included in it and not (as in the original printing) abbreviated versions of these articles, and it will have added one or two later articles which are of exactly the same character as those included by Keynes in his original collection. In the case of *Essays in Biography*, we shall add various other biographical studies that Keynes wrote throughout his work.

There will follow three volumes, XI to XIV, of economic articles and correspondence, and one volume of social, political and literary writings. We shall include in these volumes such part of Keynes's economic correspondence as is closely associated with the articles that are printed in them.

The further nine volumes, as we estimate at present, will deal with Keynes's *Activities* during the years from the beginning of his public life in 1905 until his death. In each of the periods into which we propose to divide this material, the volume concerned will publish his more ephemeral writings, all of it hitherto un-collected, his correspondence relating to these activities, and such other material and correspondence as is necessary to the understanding of Keynes's activities. The first four of these volumes are being edited by Elizabeth Johnson; the later volumes will be the responsibility of Donald Moggridge. It is their task to trace and interpret Keynes's activities sufficiently to make the material fully intelligible to a later generation. Until this work has progressed further, it is not possible to say with exactitude whether this material will be distributed, as we now think, over nine volumes, or whether it will need to be spread over a further volume or volumes. There will be a final volume of bibliography and index.

Those responsible for this edition have been: Lord Kahn, both as Lord Keynes's executor and as a long and intimate friend of Lord Keynes, able to help in the interpreting of much that would otherwise be misunderstood; Sir Roy Harrod as the author of his biography; Austin Robinson as Keynes's co-editor on the *Economic Journal* and successor as secretary of the Royal Economic Society. The initial editorial tasks were carried by Elizabeth Johnson. More recently she has been joined in this responsibility by Donald Moggridge. They have been assisted at different times by Jane Thistlethwaite; Mrs McDonald, who was originally responsible for the systematic ordering of the files of the Keynes papers; Judith Masterman, who for many years worked with Mrs Johnson on the papers; and more recently by Susan Wilsher and Margaret Butler.

NOTE TO THE READER

A Tract on Monetary Reform was first published in England on 11 December 1923. It was reprinted in 1924, 1929 and 1932. There were also American, French, German, Italian, Danish and Japanese editions. Of these, only the French edition had a preface differing from the English.[1]

At the bottom of the final page of the table of contents of the original English edition, Keynes wrote

'I have utilised, mainly in the first chapter and in parts of the second and third, the material, much revised and re-written, of some articles which were published during 1922 in the Reconstruction Supplements of the *Manchester Guardian Commercial*.'

The articles in question and their dates of publication were: 'The Theory of the Exchanges and "Purchasing Power Parity"', 20 April 1922; 'The Forward Market in Foreign Exchanges', 20 April 1922; 'Inflation as a Method of Taxation', 27 July 1922; 'The Consequences to Society of Changes in the Value of Money', 27 July 1922.

The existence of these articles posed a problem for the editors. If we had reproduced the articles separately, it would have meant considerable duplication in so far as they also appear in the *Tract*. In one case, moreover, given the reprinting of much of chapter 1 of the *Tract* in *Essays in Persuasion* (volume IX), it would have implied triplication. If, on the other hand, we had reproduced the *Tract* as originally printed but made reference to the changes that occurred since the publication of the relevant articles over a year before, we would have run the risk of distracting the readers with a large number of footnotes. This method, however, had the added advantage that we could have provided an example of how Keynes moved material between

[1] The Italian edition, translated by Mr Piero Sraffa, left out the last sentence of the English preface in translation.

media and audiences and also indicate how his views evolved over time. Given this advantage, after experimenting with this approach, we have decided to adopt it.

The text reproduced here is basically that of the first printing of the *Tract*. However, we have removed the excessive capitalisation favoured by his original printers, made the minor corrections indicated in Keynes's working copy of the volume,[1] added the French preface and introduced into chapter 1 some contemporary cartoons which Keynes chose to accompany the version printed in the *Manchester Guardian Commercial*. In footnotes we indicate all changes from the articles of the previous year other than those resulting from the updating of tables on the correction of figures. Keynes's footnotes in the *Tract* are set off in square brackets in the sections where the articles and the final text are compared.

[1] These are noted in Appendix III.

PREFACE

We leave saving to the private investor, and we encourage him to place his savings mainly in titles to money. We leave the responsibility for setting production in motion to the business man, who is mainly influenced by the profits which he expects to accrue to himself in terms of money. Those who are not in favour of drastic changes in the existing organisation of society believe that these arrangements, being in accord with human nature, have great advantages. But they cannot work properly if the money, which they assume as a stable measuring-rod, is undependable. Unemployment, the precarious life of the worker, the disappointment of expectation, the sudden loss of savings, the excessive windfalls to individuals, the speculator, the profiteer —all proceed, in large measure, from the instability of the standard of value.

It is often supposed that the costs of production are threefold, corresponding to the rewards of labour, enterprise, and accumulation. But there is a fourth cost, namely risk; and the reward of risk-bearing is one of the heaviest, and perhaps the most avoidable, burden on production. This element of risk is greatly aggravated by the instability of the standard of value. Currency reforms, which led to the adoption by this country and the world at large of sound monetary principles, would diminish the wastes of *risk*, which consume at present too much of our estate.

Nowhere do conservative notions consider themselves more in place than in currency; yet nowhere is the need of innovation more urgent. One is often warned that a scientific treatment of currency questions is impossible because the banking world is intellectually incapable of understanding its own problems. If this is true, the order of society, which they stand for, will decay. But I do not believe it. What we have lacked is a clear analysis of the real facts, rather than ability to understand an analysis already given. If the new ideas, now developing in many quarters, are sound and right, I do not doubt that sooner or later they will prevail. I dedicate this book, humbly and without permission, to the Governors and Court of the Bank of England, who now and for the future have a much more difficult and anxious task entrusted to them than in former days.

J. M. KEYNES

October 1923

PREFACE TO THE FRENCH EDITION

Events in the world of money move fast; but it does not follow that principles shift as quickly. In addressing this edition to the French public, I may be excused, therefore, if I seek to apply, in a few words, the principles of this book to the changes which have come over the financial situation of France during the past six months.

I have maintained for a long time that a substantial fall in the value of the franc was inevitable unless there was to be a more drastic change in the policy of the French Treasury than was likely to be politically feasible. This fall has now taken place. The effect of the fall on the mind of the public is to engender increased distrust and fear, and the atmosphere is pessimistic. Nevertheless the establishment of financial equilibrium is easier now than it was before the fall took place.

Let me first clear out of the way certain opinions and arguments, which appear in the past to have influenced opinion, yet are altogether contrary to good sense:

1. It has never been officially admitted that the value of the franc can ever be fixed at any other value, either in gold or in commodities, than its pre-war gold parity. This is absurd. A restoration of the pre-war gold parity, apart from other intolerable consequences, would increase fourfold the present burden of the French National Debt. It is easy to calculate that the holders of the debt would have a claim in that event practically equal to the entire wealth of France. No Finance Minister there ever was could balance such a budget. Unless, therefore, the franc is *never* to be stabilised, in terms either of gold or of commodities, this figment of an ultimate return to a pre-war parity must be discarded.

2. Whenever the franc falls in value, the Minister of Finance is convinced that this is due to anything except economic causes and attributes it to the presence of a foreigner in the neighbour-

hood of the Bourse or to the mysterious and malignant influences of 'speculation'. This is not far removed, intellectually, from an African witch doctor's ascription of cattle disease to the 'evil eye' of a bystander or of bad weather to the unsatisfied appetites of an idol.

In the first place the volume of speculation, properly so called, is always extremely small in proportion to the volume of normal business. In the second place the successful speculator makes his profit by anticipating, not by modifying, existing economic tendencies. In the third place, most speculation, especially 'bear' speculation, is for very short periods of time, so that the closing of the transaction soon exerts an influence equal and opposite to its initial effect. Moreover there has probably been on balance, since the date of the Armistice, more speculation in favour of the franc than against it. At least I can testify that many Englishmen, and even more Americans, have lost large sums by purchasing francs or franc investments in the hope of profiting from an improvement in the value of the franc.

I beg the attention of French readers to the arguments of chapters 2 and 3 of this book, because superstitions about speculation can only exist in an atmosphere of ignorance concerning the veritable influences which fix the level of the exchanges. In estimating lightly the influence of speculation, I do not include, however, the effects of a general distrust of the future prospects of a currency, to which I refer later.

3. It is often argued that the franc cannot fall in value because France is a wealthy, thrifty and industrious country, or because her balance of trade is *prima facie* satisfactory. This again springs from confusion as to the causes which ultimately govern the value of money. A very rich country can have a very bad currency, and a very poor country a very good one. The wealth of France and her balance of trade may render it easier for her authorities to pursue a sound monetary policy. But they are not the same thing. The value of a country's monetary unit is not a function of its wealth or even of its trade balance.

What, then, has determined and will determine the value of the franc? First, the quantity, present and prospective, of the francs in circulation. Second, the amount of purchasing power which it suits the public to hold in that shape. (The quantity theory in the form in which I state it in the first section of chapter 3, below, may, I think, be novel to many French readers.) The first of these two elements, namely the quantity of the currency, depends mainly on the loan and budgetary policies of the French Treasury. The second of them depends mainly (in present conditions) on the trust or distrust which the public feel in the prospects of the value of the franc.

With the franc in the neighbourhood of 120 to the £ sterling, the former task does not appear to the outside observer to be unduly difficult. When the internal price level has adjusted itself to the exchanges, the yield of many of the existing taxes in terms of paper francs will naturally be increased. On the other hand, the biggest item of expenditure, namely the service of the internal debt, will remain the same as before. Thus, even apart from additional taxation, the mere movement of the exchange has in itself a tendency to restore the budget towards equilibrium; provided always that public faith is maintained in the prospects of the national currency.

It is in this second factor, therefore, that the crux of the situation lies, namely the attitude of the French public towards their own currency. I emphasise the fact that the matter lies in the hands of Frenchmen themselves, not in those of any foreign persons. For the amount of francs owned by foreigners is probably not very great, not much more than what is still left in their hands as the remnant of disappointed 'bull' operations; and the obstacles are insuperable to 'bear' sales by foreigners of francs, which they do not possess, on a really large scale. On the other hand the volume of franc-notes and franc-bills and other short-dated investments held in France itself is enormous, far beyond the minimum required for the convenient transaction of business. If Frenchmen get it into their heads (as, each in their turn, Russians, Austrians and Germans have done) that their national legal-tender money and titles to legal-tender represent a depreciating asset, then there is no near limit to the fall in the value of the franc. For, in this event, they will diminish their holdings of such assets; they will keep fewer Bank of France notes in their pocket-books and in their safes, will liquidate their *Bons de Trésor* and will sell their *rentes*. No law or regulation will avail to restrain them. Moreover the process will be cumulative; for each successive liquidation of franc assets and their transference into 'real values', by provoking a further fall, will seem to justify the prescience of those who fled first from the franc and will thus prepare the way for a second outburst of distrust.

In this case the fall of the franc will not be prevented even by a reformed budget or a favourable surplus of trade. For it would be necessary for the government to absorb the redundant banknotes and franc-bonds and -bills, which the public no longer cared to hold, a task unavoidably beyond the government's power. We have the experience of many countries to demonstrate that unbalanced budgets are the initial cause of collapse, but that the real *dégringolade* only comes when the confidence of the general public is so far undermined that they begin to contract their holdings of the legal-tender money.

The central task of the French government at this moment is, therefore, to preserve confidence in the franc in the minds of the widest circles of the French public. For it is the failure of this internal confidence, not speculation by foreigners (though foreigners and Frenchmen too may take advantage of a collapsing currency to win great gains), which would prove their undoing.

Now, if they go the right way about it, there is nothing impossible in the task of restoring and maintaining confidence. The examples of Russia, Austria and Germany are not a just parallel. Those who foresee the future of the franc in the light of such previous experiences may make a big mistake. For in those countries the problem of balancing the budget was, during the earlier phases, a virtual impossibility. The initial impulse towards collapse was, therefore, also a continuing impulse. This is not so in France. There is no impossibility in achieving a fiscal equilibrium, provided that reconstruction expenditure is reasonably postponed. I applaud the efforts of M. Poincaré and the French Treasury in this direction. But this is not enough by itself. It is also necessary to restore public confidence; and in this sphere of action every step taken by M. de Lasteyrie has been away from wisdom.

For upon what foundations does the credit of a currency rest? They are much the same as with a bank. A bank can only attract and retain the deposits of its clients, so long as these clients possess a complete confidence in their freedom to withdraw these deposits for exchange into other assets, if they have a mind to do so. As long as this liberty is beyond doubt, it will not be exercised; the deposits will rest and grow. But if it is once called in question, they will shrink and disappear. So is it with a currency. Men hold a part of their resources in money, because they believe it to be more readily and freely interchangeable than any alternative hoard, into whatsoever object of value they may select hereafter. If this belief proves wrong, they will not hold money and nothing can make them do so.

Now the prime object of most of M. de Lasteyrie's regulations is to restrict the liberty of holders of francs to exchange them at their discretion into other forms of value. So far, therefore, from protecting the franc and restoring its credit, they are directly calculated to shatter confidence and to destroy its credit. A sufficient number of regulations would destroy the value, precisely because they would destroy the utility, of any currency in the world. As soon as there is a doubt as to whether francs (or *Bons de Trésor*) are a truly liquid asset, these instruments cease to serve the purpose for which they are held, and holders hasten to dispose of them before the doubt is resolved into a certainty and yet further obstacles can have been placed in the way.

An instructive example of the way in which regulations produce the opposite effect to that which they intend is given by those of which the object is to hinder speculative operations. Those who have opened, in one way or another, a 'bear' position against the currency in question are in no way perturbed; for they can reckon with confidence that it will always be possible for them to *buy* the currency which in due course they will require to cover their open position. Those, on the other hand, who have taken up a 'bull' position and will, therefore, require to *sell* the currency at some later date, are thrown into confusion and seek in haste to sell their interest while still they may. It is for this reason that the threat of interference with the freedom of exchange dealings invariably operates to depress the value of the currency which it is sought to regulate. Just as a man draws out his deposits at the bank, whether he needs the money or not, as soon as he has reason to believe that he may not be free to do so later on, so the general public and the financial world alike withdraw their resources from a currency, if they fear a limitation on their subsequent freedom of withdrawal.

What course then should the French Treasury now take in face of the dangers surrounding them? It is soon said. First the government must so strengthen its fiscal position that its power to control the volume of the currency is beyond doubt, the necessity of which is at least accepted. Secondly—and especially during the interval which must needs elapse before the first category of measures can be brought into full operation—the government must restore such complete confidence in the liberty of the franc that no one will think it worth while to enter by way of precaution into sales of francs not immediately urgent—the equal necessity of which seems to be overlooked.

To achieve this latter object nothing more is required than a reversal of the recent policy of restrictions on dealing, of the useless hoarding of gold, of a relatively low bank rate, and of secrecy about the actual position of the Treasury and the Bank of France. The chief measures which are necessary can be summarised under three heads:

1. All limitations on the use of francs to purchase foreign currencies, foreign bonds, or goods, whether for immediate or for deferred delivery, should be wholly repealed.

2. The discount rate of the Bank of France should be raised to a high figure, probably not less than 10 per cent in present circumstances (though it might not be necessary to maintain such a high rate for any length of time), so as to counteract anticipations, well- or ill-founded, as to the possible depreciation of the franc. In view of the high rate of interest now obtainable on French government securities (let alone the rates on forward exchange) the present rate of discount does not correspond to the facts of the situation and is calculated to stimulate overborrowing. Possibly some increase of the Bank of France's rate may have been effected by the time these lines are in print.

3. A considerable sum, drawn from the still ample gold reserve of the Bank of France, should be made the basis of a foreign credit, either by outright sale or by borrowing against it, to be available for use without stint in supporting the exchange near the present level and restoring confidence during the interval before fiscal reforms can produce their full effect.

I warrant that these simple well-tried measures, in combination with political moderation and with the drastic economies and taxes, without which no other measures can finally avail, would have a marvellous efficacy. After a few weeks of this medicine and with a benevolent reception by M. Poincaré (or his successor) of the forthcoming Experts' Reports, the franc would be as steady as a rock. But if, on the other hand, distrust in the franc is countered by the methods of the Holy Inquisition, if Frenchmen prefer the concealed capital levy of inflation to other forms of taxation, if France remains the trouble-peace of Europe, then the franc may follow the course of other once-noble tokens.

March 1924   J. M. KEYNES

Chapter 1[1]

THE CONSEQUENCES
TO SOCIETY OF CHANGES IN THE
VALUE OF MONEY

Money is only important for what it will procure. Thus a change
in the monetary unit, which is uniform in its operation and affects
all transactions equally, has no consequences. If, by a change in
the established standard of value, a man received and owned
twice as much money as he did before in payment for all rights
and for all efforts, and if he also paid out twice as much money
for all acquisitions and for all satisfactions, he would be wholly
unaffected.

It follows, therefore, that a change in the value of money, that
is to say in the level of prices, is important to society only in so
far as its incidence is unequal. Such changes have produced in
the past, and are producing now, the vastest social consequences,
because, as we all know, when the value of money changes, it
does *not* change equally for all persons or for all purposes.
A man's receipts and his outgoings are not all modified in one
uniform proportion. Thus a change in prices and rewards, as
measured in money, generally affects different classes unequally,
transfers wealth from one to another, bestows affluence here and
embarrassment there, and redistributes Fortune's favours so as
to frustrate design and disappoint expectation.

The fluctuations in the value of money since 1914 have been
on a scale so great as to constitute, with all that they involve, one
of the most significant events in the economic history of the
modern world. The fluctuation of the standard, whether gold,
silver, or paper, has not only been of unprecedented violence,

[1] This chapter follows the article of the same title dated 27 July 1922, unless otherwise
noted.

I

but has[1] been visited on a society of which the economic organisation[2] is more dependent than that of any earlier epoch on the assumption that the standard of value would be moderately stable.

During the Napoleonic Wars and the period immediately succeeding them the extreme fluctuation of English prices within a single year was 22 per cent; and the highest price level reached during the first quarter of the nineteenth century, which we used to reckon the most disturbed period of our currency history, was less than double the lowest[3] and with an interval of thirteen years. Compare with this the extraordinary movements of the past nine years. To recall the reader's mind to the exact facts, I refer him to the table on the next page.

I have not included those countries—Russia, Poland, and Austria—where the old currency has long been[4] bankrupt. But it will be observed that, even[5] apart from the countries which have suffered revolution or defeat, no quarter of the world has escaped a violent movement. In the United States, where the gold standard has functioned unabated, in Japan, where the war brought with it more profit than liability, in the neutral country of Sweden, the changes in the value of money have been comparable with those in the United Kingdom.

From[6] 1914 to 1920 all these countries experienced an expansion in the supply of money to spend relatively to the supply of things to purchase, that is to say *inflation*. Since 1920 those countries which have regained control of their financial situation, not content with bringing the inflation to an end, have contracted their supply of money and have experienced the fruits of *deflation*. Others have followed inflationary courses more riotously

---

[1] In the article, the beginning of this sentence reads: 'The fluctuation of the standard has not only shown unprecedented violence, gold, silver, and paper alike, and in all countries, but it has'.

[2] In the article, the words between 'organisation' and 'epoch' ran 'was peculiarly dependent as compared with that of any earlier epoch'.

[3] In the article, the rest of the sentence ran 'and at an interval of thirteen years from it'.

[4] The words 'has long been' in the text replace the word 'is' in the article.

[5] The word 'even' in the text replaces the word 'quite' in the article.

[6] The remaining paragraphs of this section are peculiar to the *Tract*.

*Index numbers of wholesale prices expressed as a
percentage of 1913*[1]

Monthly average	United Kingdom[2]	France	Italy	Germany	U.S.A.[3]	Canada	Japan	Sweden	India
1913	100	100	100	100	100	100	100	100	—
1914	100	102	96	106	98	100	95	116	100
1915	127	140	133	142	101	109	97	145	112
1916	160	189	201	153	127	134	117	185	128
1917	206	262	299	179	177	175	149	244	147
1918	227	340	409	217	194	205	196	339	180
1919	242	357	364	415	206	216	239	330	198
1920	295	510	624	1,486	226	250	260	347	204
1921	182	345	577	1,911	147	182	200	211	181
1922	159	327	562	34,182	149	165	196	162	180
1923[4]	159	411	582	765,000	157	167	192	166	179

[1] These figures are taken from the *Monthly Bulletin of Statistics* of the League of Nations.
[2] *Statist* up to 1919; thereafter the median of the *Economist*, *Statist*, and Board of Trade index numbers.
[3] Bureau of Labour index number (revised).
[4] First half-year.

than before. In a few, of which Italy is one, an imprudent desire to deflate has been balanced by the intractability of the financial situation, with the happy result of comparatively stable prices.

Each process, inflation and deflation alike, has inflicted great injuries. Each has an effect in altering the *distribution* of wealth between different classes, inflation in this respect being the worse of the two. Each has also an effect in overstimulating or retarding the *production* of wealth, though here deflation is the more injurious. The division of our subject thus indicated is the most convenient for us to follow, examining first the effect of changes in the value of money on the distribution of wealth with most of our attention on inflation, and next their effect on the production of wealth with most of our attention on deflation. How have the price changes of the past nine years affected the productivity of the community as a whole, and how have they affected the conflicting interests and mutual relations of its component classes? The answer to these questions will serve to establish the gravity of the evils, into the remedy for which it is the object of this book to enquire.

I. CHANGES IN THE VALUE OF MONEY
AS AFFECTING DISTRIBUTION

For the purpose of this enquiry[1] a triple classification of society is convenient—into the investing class, the business class, and the earning class. These classes overlap, and the same individual may earn, deal, and invest; but in the present organisation of society such a division corresponds to a social cleavage and an actual divergence of interest.[2]

1. *The investing class*

Of the various purposes which money serves, some essentially depend upon the assumption that its real value is nearly constant over a period of time. The chief of these are those connected, in a wide sense, with contracts for the *investment of money*. Such contracts—namely, those which provide for the payment of fixed sums of money over a long period of time—are the characteristic of what it is convenient to call the *investment system*, as distinct from the property system generally.

Under this phase of capitalism, as developed during the nine-teenth century,[3] many arrangements were devised for separating the management of property from its ownership. These arrange-ments were of three leading types: (1) those in which the proprietor, while parting with the management of his property, retained his ownership of it—i.e. of the actual land, buildings, and machinery, or of whatever else it consisted in, this mode of

---

[1] In the article the words 'into the varying social incidence of a change in the value of money' are added.

[2] In the original article the following sentences concluded this paragraph: 'How have the price changes of the past eight years affected the interests and mutual relations of these components? If we could answer this question accurately and well, we should have begun to interpret the subterranean forces which to-day are shaking Europe.'

[3] In the article the following words were inserted between 'century' and 'many': 'which I thus describe as the *investment system*'.

tenure being[1] typified by a holding of ordinary shares in a joint-stock company; (2) those in which he parted with the property temporarily, receiving a fixed sum of *money* annually in the meantime, but regained his property eventually, as[2] typified by a lease; and (3) those in which he parted with his real property permanently, in return either for a perpetual annuity fixed in terms of money, or for a terminable annuity and the repayment of the principal in money at the end of the term, as[3] typified by mortgages, bonds, debentures, and preference shares. This third type represents the full development of *investment*.

Contracts to receive fixed sums of money at future dates (made without provision for possible changes in the real value of money at those dates) must have existed as long as money has been lent and borrowed. In the form of leases and mortgages, and also of permanent loans to governments and[4] to a few private bodies, such as the East India Company, they were already frequent[5] in the eighteenth century. But during the nineteenth century they developed a new and increased[6] importance, and had, by the beginning of the twentieth, divided the propertied classes into two groups—the 'business men' and the 'investors'—with partly divergent interests. The division was not sharp as between individuals: for business men might be investors also, and investors might hold ordinary shares; but the division was nevertheless real,[7] and not the less important because it was seldom noticed.[8]

By this system the active business class could call to the aid of their enterprises not only their own wealth but the savings of the whole community; and the professional and propertied classes,

[1] The words 'this mode of tenure being' do not appear in the article.
[2] The word 'as' was omitted in the article.
[3] 'As' in the text replaces the words 'these being' in the article.
[4] The words 'to a few private bodies, such as' in the text replace the words 'to such bodies (few in number) as' in the article.
[5] The word 'frequent' in the text replaces the words 'becoming important' in the article.
[6] The words 'a new and increased' in the text replace the words 'an entirely novel' in the article.
[7] The word 'real' in the text replaces the words 'a real one' in the article.
[8] The words 'seldom noticed' in the text replace the words 'largely unobserved' in the article.

on the other hand, could find an employment for their resources, which involved them in little trouble, no responsibility and (it was believed) small risk.

For a hundred years the system worked, throughout Europe,[1] with an extraordinary[2] success and facilitated the growth of wealth on an unprecedented scale.[3] To save and to invest became at once the duty and the delight of a large class. The savings were seldom drawn on, and, accumulating at compound interest, made possible the material triumphs which we now all take for granted. The morals, the politics, the literature, and the religion of the age joined in a grand conspiracy for the promotion of saving.[4] God and Mammon were reconciled. Peace on earth to men of good means. A rich man could, after all, enter into the Kingdom of Heaven—if only he saved. A new harmony sounded from the celestial spheres. 'It is curious to observe how, through the wise and beneficent arrangement of Providence, men thus do the greatest service to the public, when they are thinking of nothing but their own gain';[5] so sang the angels.

The[6] atmosphere thus created well harmonised the demands of expanding business and the needs of an expanding population with the growth of a comfortable non-business class. But amidst the general enjoyment of ease and progress, the extent to which the system depended on the stability of the money to which the investing classes had committed their fortunes was generally

---

[1] The words 'throughout Europe' are peculiar to the text.

[2] The word 'extraordinary' in the text replaces the words 'almost incredible' in the article.

[3] The words 'an unprecedented scale' in the text replace the words 'a scale entirely unprecedented' in the article.

[4] In the article, the following sentences were added at this point: 'Was there any other duty so assiduously implanted in the infant breast? Or any worse immorality, than to live on one's capital, in the catalogue of adult crimes?'

[5] [*Easy Lessons on Money Matters for the Use of Young People*. Published by the Society for Promoting Christian Knowledge. Twelfth Edition, 1850.]

[6] The material contained in this paragraph and in the first sentence of the succeeding paragraph are peculiar to the *Tract* at this point. They replace the following paragraph in the article:

'Yet what was this money to which the investing classes had committed their fortunes? A certain quantity of gold?—not even this, except for so long as the law of the land might thus define it. Money is the child (or the changeling) of the State, and is simply that which is declared by the State from time to time to be a good legal discharge of money contracts.'

THE HOUSING QUESTION.
" The man who asked a house agent if he had a house to let."
(J. M. Bateman, 1919)

[Reproduced by permission of PUNCH]

overlooked; and an unquestioning confidence was apparently felt that this matter would look after itself. Investments spread and multiplied, until, for the middle classes of the world, the gilt-edged bond came to typify all that was most permanent and most secure. So rooted in our day has been the conventional belief in the stability and safety of a money contract that, according to English law, trustees have been encouraged to embark their trust funds exclusively in such transactions, and are indeed forbidden, except in the case of real estate (an exception which is itself a survival of the conditions of an earlier age), to employ them otherwise.[1]

---

[1] [German trustees were not released from a similar obligation until 1923, by which date the value of trust funds invested in titles to money had entirely disappeared.]

As in other respects, so also in this, the nineteenth century relied on the future permanence of its own happy experiences and disregarded the warning of past misfortunes. It chose to forget that[1] there is no historical warrant for expecting money to be represented even by a constant quantity of a particular metal, far less by a constant purchasing power. Yet money is simply that which the State declares from time to time to be a good legal discharge of money contracts.[2] In 1914 gold had not been the English standard for a century or the sole standard of any other country for half a century. There is no record of a prolonged war or a great social upheaval which has not been accompanied by a change in the legal tender, but[3] an almost unbroken chronicle in every country which has a history, back to the earliest dawn of economic record, of a progressive deterioration in the real value of the successive legal tenders which have represented money.[4]

Moreover,[5] this progressive deterioration in the value of money through history is not an accident, and has had behind it two great driving forces—the impecuniosity of governments and the superior political influence of the debtor class.

The power of taxation by currency depreciation is one which has been inherent in the State since Rome discovered it. The creation of legal tender has been and is a government's ultimate

---

[1] The words 'It chose to forget that' are peculiar to the text.

[2] The preceding sentence is peculiar to the text at this point.

[3] In the article 'but' begins a new sentence and is followed by the additional words 'above all, there is' before 'an'.

[4] In the article a sentence is added to the text. 'Every schoolboy knows how a sheep once cost fourpence.'

[5] The next two paragraphs in the text replace the following paragraph in the article:

'This progressive deterioration in the value of money through history has had behind it two great driving forces—the impecuniosity of governments and the political influence of the debtor class. The power of creating legal tender at a profit is one which is and always has been inherent in the monarch or in the State, and it has never not been abused. A state at war, or a government dependent for its office upon profusion must needs require more money than legitimate methods can afford; and sooner or later every governing authority is subjected to one of these contingencies. Yet when so placed no state or government is likely to decree its own bankruptcy or its own downfall, so long as the instrument of currency depreciation still lies at hand unused. A depreciation of the currency has been and is a government's ultimate reserve; and even in the most respectable quarters a draft on the reserve may be expected once in a century.'

reserve; and no state or government is likely to decree its own bankruptcy or its own downfall, so long as this instrument still lies at hand unused.

Besides this,[1] we shall see below, the benefits of a depreciating currency are not restricted to the government. Farmers and debtors and all persons liable to pay fixed money dues share in the advantage. As now in the persons of business men, so also in former ages these classes constituted the active and constructive elements in the economic scheme. Those secular changes, therefore, which in the past have depreciated money, assisted the new men and emancipated them from the dead hand; they benefited new wealth at the expense of old, and armed enterprise against accumulation. The tendency of money to depreciate has been in past times a weighty counterpoise against the cumulative results of compound interest and the inheritance of fortunes. It has been a loosening influence against the rigid distribution of old-won wealth and the separation of ownership from activity. By this means each generation can disinherit in part its predecessors' heirs; and the project of founding a perpetual fortune[2] must be disappointed in this way, unless the community with conscious deliberation provides against it in some other way, more equitable and more expedient.

At[3] any rate, under the influence of these two forces—the

---

[1] The words 'besides this' in the text replace the word 'but' in the article.
[2] The rest of the paragraph in the text replaces the words 'is disappointed' in the article.
[3] The next two paragraphs in the text replace the following two paragraphs from the article, the first sentence of which appeared on page 7 above:

'Yet so rooted in our day is the conventional belief in the stability and safety of a money contract that, according to English law, trustees have been encouraged to embark their trust funds exclusively in such transactions, and are indeed largely precluded, except in the case of land (an exception which is itself a survival of the conditions of an earlier age) from employing them otherwise. Investments have spread and multiplied; and for the middle classes of the world the gilt-edged bond came to typify all that was most permanent and most secure in the transitory adventure of existence.

'Looked at coolly and objectively (and in the light of current events) the confidence shown in so curious a construction must seem remarkable to the philosophical observer. It is attributable to more than one influence. The ordinary man had learnt, as a natural consequence of the habitual use of money in all the transactions of his daily life (rapidly though he is now unlearning it) to look on money as itself the absolute standard of value and to forget any more ultimate standard behind it, based on the real criterion of human satisfactions. But, besides this, the actual events of the nineteenth century had not dis-

9

financial necessities of governments and the political influence of the debtor class—sometimes the one and sometimes the other, the progress of inflation has been *continuous,* if we consider long periods, ever since money was first devised in the sixth century B.C. Sometimes the standard of value has depreciated of itself; failing this, debasements have done the work.

Nevertheless it is easy at all times, as a result of the way we use money in daily life, to forget all this and to look on money as itself the absolute standard of value; and when, besides, the actual events of a hundred years have not disturbed his illusions, the average man regards what has been normal for three generations as a part of the permanent social fabric.

The course of events during the nineteenth century favoured such ideas.[1] During its first quarter,[2] the very high prices of the Napoleonic Wars were followed by a somewhat rapid improvement in the value of money. For the next seventy years, with some contemporary fluctuations, the tendency of prices continued to be downwards, the lowest point being reached in 1896. But while this was the tendency as regards direction, the remarkable feature of this long period was the relative *stability* of the price level. Approximately the *same* level of price ruled in or about the years 1826, 1841, 1855, 1862, 1867, 1871, and 1915. Prices were also level in the years 1844, 1881, and 1914. If we call the index number of these latter years 100, we find that, for the period of close on a century from 1826 to the outbreak of war, the maximum fluctuation in either direction was 30 points, the index number never rising above 130 and never falling below 70. No wonder that we came to believe in the stability of money contracts over a long period. The metal *gold* might not possess all

turbed his illusions, and in the mind of man, whose memory is shorter even than his own life, what has been normal for three generations becomes, for him, a part of the permanent social fabric.'

[1] The words 'such ideas' in the text replace the words 'to a singular degree a development along such lines' in the article.

[2] The sequence of words 'the very high prices of the Napoleonic Wars, were followed' in the text replaced the words 'the Napoleonic wars, a period of very high prices, were followed by a somewhat rapid fall of prices, or, in other words,'.

the theoretical advantages of an artificially regulated standard, but[1] it could not be tampered with and had proved[2] reliable in practice.

At[3] the same time, the investor in Consols in the early part of the century had done very well[4] in three different ways. The 'security' of his investment[5] had come to be considered as near absolute perfection as was possible. Its capital value had uniformly appreciated, partly for the reason just stated, but chiefly because the steady fall in the rate of interest increased the number of years' purchase of the annual income which represented the capital.[6] And the annual money income had a purchasing power which on the whole was increasing. If, for example, we consider the seventy years from 1826 to 1896 (and ignore the great improvement immediately after Waterloo), we find that the capital value of Consols rose steadily, with only temporary set-backs, from 79 to 109 (in spite of Goschen's conversion from a 3 per cent rate to a $2\frac{3}{4}$ per cent rate in 1889 and a $2\frac{1}{2}$ per cent rate effective in 1903), while the purchasing power of the annual dividends, even after allowing for the reduced rates of interest, had increased 50 per cent. But[7] Consols, too,[8] had added the virtue of stability to that of improvement. Except in years of crisis Consols never fell below 90 during the reign of Queen Victoria; and even in '48, when thrones were crumbling, the

[1] In the text the words 'at least' were deleted from the article.
[2] The words 'reliable in practice' in the text replace the words 'its reliability by experience' in the article.
[3] This sentence in the text follows an additional sentence in the article which ran as follows: 'The conventional wisdom of one generation being based on the experience of its predecessor, we have here an abundantly adequate explanation of the reputation which at the end of the nineteenth century the "gilt-edged" investment had secured.' The words 'At the same time' in the text did not appear in the article.
[4] In the text the words 'for himself—very well for three different reasons and' were deleted from the article.
[5] In the text the words '(as judged by the investment market) had steadily improved and' were deleted from the article.
[6] [If (for example) the rate of interest falls from $4\frac{1}{2}$ per cent to 3 per cent, 3 per cent Consols rise in value from 66 to 100.]
[7] In the text, the following footnote was deleted from the article: 'Thus the purchasing power of the capital value—in the event of the investor wishing to realise his capital—had more than doubled.'
[8] In the text, the word 'too' was added to the article.

mean price of the year fell but 5 points. Ninety when she ascended the throne, they reached their maximum with her in the year of Diamond Jubilee.[1] What wonder that our parents thought Consols a good investment!

Thus there grew up during the nineteenth century a large, powerful,[2] and greatly[2] respected class of persons, well-to-do individually and very wealthy in the aggregate, who owned neither buildings, nor land, nor businesses, nor precious metals, but titles to an annual income in legal-tender money. In particular, that peculiar creation and pride of the nineteenth century, the savings of the middle class, had been mainly[3] thus embarked. Custom and favourable experience had acquired for such[4] investments[5] an unimpeachable reputation for security.

Before the war these medium fortunes had already begun to suffer some loss (as compared with the summit of their prosperity in the middle nineties) from the rise in prices and also in the rate of interest. But the monetary events which have accompanied and have followed the war have taken from them about one-half of their real value in England, seven-eighths[6] in France, eleven-twelfths in Italy, and[7] virtually the whole in Germany and in the succession states of Austria-Hungary and Russia.

The[8] loss to the typical English investor of the pre-war period

---

[1] In the text, the following sentence was deleted from the article: 'Other gilt-edged stocks had moved similarly'.

[2] In the text the word 'a' was deleted from the article before this word.

[3] The word 'mainly' in the text replaces the word 'largely' in the article.

[4] The word 'such' in the text replaces the word 'these' in the article.

[5] The words 'an unimpeachable reputation for security' in the text replace the words 'a reputation for security supposedly almost absolute' in the article.

[6] The word 'seven-eighths' in the text replaces the word 'six-sevenths' in the article.

[7] The rest of the paragraph in the text replaces the following in the article: 'ninety-nine-hundredths in Germany. This apart from the increased burden of taxation.'

[8] This sentence in the text follows the following additional material in the article:
'Such a reversal of fortune deserves examination in detail. The owner of an annuity fixed in terms of money (for this is the position of the typical investor in gilt-edged securities) is exposed to two kinds of loss—a loss of capital if an annuity comes to be worth a smaller number of years' purchase of the annual income than before, and a loss of purchasing power if money falls in value. If both these tendencies are at work, his loss, in the event of his wishing to realise the investment, is a double one—his security sells for less money, and each unit of the money for which it sells is worth less.'

"LET ME FIX THE WORLD'S PRICES : I CARE NOT WHO MAKES ITS LAWS."

Will Dyson

Courtesy of I.P.C. Newspapers

is sufficiently measured by the loss to the investor in Consols. Such an investor, as we have already seen, was steadily improving his position, apart from temporary fluctuations, up to 1896, and in this and the following year two maxima were reached simultaneously—both the capital value of an annuity and also the purchasing power of money. Between 1896 and 1914, on the other hand, the investor had already suffered a serious loss—the capital value of his annuity had fallen by about a third, and the purchasing power of his income had also fallen by nearly a third. This loss, however, was incurred gradually over a period of nearly twenty years from an exceptional maximum,[1] and did not leave him appreciably worse off than he had been in the early eighties or the early forties. But[2] upon the top of this came the further swifter loss of the war period. Between 1914 and 1920 the capital value of the investor's annuity again fell by more than a third, and the purchasing power of his income by about two-thirds. In addition,[3] the standard rate of income tax rose from $7\frac{1}{2}$ per cent in 1914 to 30 per cent in 1921.[4] Roughly[5] estimated in round numbers, the change may be represented thus in terms of an index of which the base year is 1914:

The second column well illustrates what a splendid investment gilt-edged stocks had been through the century from Waterloo to Mons, even if we omit altogether the abnormal values of 1896–7. Our table shows how the epoch of Diamond Jubilee was the culminating moment in[6] the prosperity of the British middle class. But it also exhibits with the precision of figures the familiar bewailed plight of those who try to live on the income of the same trustee investments as before the war. The

---

[1] The words 'from an exceptional maximum' in the text replace the words 'from a high and unaccustomed maximum' in the article where these words preceded the word 'over'.

[2] In the article the words 'there came' appeared here and the rest of the sentence followed the text with the natural exclusion of 'came'.

[3] The words 'in addition' in the text replace the words 'we have only to remember besides that' in the article.

[4] [Since 1896 there has been the further burden of the Death Duties.]

[5] The word 'roughly' in the text replaces the words 'very broadly' in the article.

[6] In the text the words 'history of' are deleted at this point from the article.

	Purchasing power of the income of Consols:[1]		Money price of the capital value of Consols	Purchasing power of the capital value of Consols
	(a) before	(b) after		
	deduction of income tax at the standard rate			
1815	61	59	92	56
1826	85	90	108	92
1841	85	90	122	104
1869	87	89	127	111
1883	104	108	138	144
1896	139	145	150	208
1914	100	100	100	100
1920	34	26	64	22
1921	53	39	56	34
1922	62	50	76	47

owner of Consols in 1922 had a real income, one half of what he had in 1914 and one third of what he had in 1896. The[2] whole of the improvement of the nineteenth century had been obliterated, and his situation was not quite so good as it had been after Waterloo.

Some mitigating circumstances should not be overlooked. Whilst the war was a period of the dissipation of the community's resources as a whole, it was a period of saving for the individuals of the saving class, who with their larger holdings of the securities of the government now have an increased aggregate money claim on the receipts of the exchequer. Also, the investing class, which has lost money, overlaps, both socially and by the ties of family, with the business class, which has made money, sufficiently to break in many cases the full severity of the loss. Moreover, in England, there has been a substantial recovery from the low point of 1920.

But these things do not wash away the significance[3] of the

[1] [Without allowance for the reduction of the interest from 3 to 2½ per cent.]

[2] This sentence replaces the following sentence in the article: 'It depicts for us how the experience of one generation may mislead another, and what a bad end awaits the too docile offspring of the wisest parent.'

[3] The words 'wash away the significance' in the text replace the words 'obliterate the character' in the article.

facts. The effect of the war, and of the monetary policy which has accompanied and followed it, has been to take away a large part of the real value of the possessions of the investing class. The loss has been so rapid and so intermixed in the time of its occurrence with other worse losses that its full measure is not yet separately apprehended. But it has effected, nevertheless, a far-reaching change in the relative position of different classes. Throughout the Continent the pre-war savings of the middle class, so far as they were invested in bonds, mortgages, or bank deposits, have been largely or entirely wiped out. Nor can it be doubted that this experience[1] must modify[2] social psychology towards the practice of saving and investment. What was deemed most secure has proved least so. He who neither spent nor 'speculated', who made 'proper provision for his family', who sang hymns to security and observed most straitly the morals of the edified and the respectable injunctions of the worldly wise—he, indeed, who gave fewest pledges to Fortune has yet suffered her heaviest visitations.

What[3] moral for our present purpose should we draw from this? Chiefly, I think, that it is not safe or fair to combine the social organisation developed during the nineteenth century (and still retained) with a *laisser-faire* policy towards the value of money. It is not true that our former arrangements have worked well. If we are to continue to draw the voluntary savings of the community into 'investments', we must make it a prime object of deliberate State policy that the standard value, in terms of which they are expressed, should be kept stable; adjusting in other ways (calculated to touch all forms of wealth equally and

[1] The words 'this experience' in the text replace the words 'the full realisation of what has happened'.
[2] The word 'modify' in the text replaces the word 'affect' in the article.
[3] This paragraph is peculiar to the text and replaces the following paragraph in the article:
'Is this deprivation a net loss to the community, or is it one side of a redistribution of wealth from which other classes have benefited? The fund of real values, of which the investing classes have been deprived, has partly accrued to the State and has been dissipated in the consumptions of war. In part, however, this wealth has been redistributed, the business classes and the working classes each gaining a share of it. A further discussion of this topic leads us to the next section of our argument.'

not concentrated on the relatively helpless 'investors') the redistribution of the national wealth, if, in course of time, the laws of inheritance and the rate of accumulation have drained too great a proportion of the income of the active classes into the spending control of the inactive.

2. *The business class*

It has long been recognised, by the business world and by economists alike, that a period of rising prices acts as a stimulus to enterprise and is beneficial to business men.

In the first place there is the advantage which is the counterpart of the loss to the investing class which we have just examined. When[1] the value of money falls, it is evident that those persons who have engaged to pay fixed sums of money yearly out of the profits of active business must benefit, since their fixed money outgoings will bear a smaller proportion than formerly to their money turnover. This benefit persists not only during the transitional period of change, but also, so far as old loans are concerned, when prices have settled down at their new and higher level. For example, the farmers throughout Europe, who had raised by mortgage the funds to purchase the land they farmed, now find themselves almost freed from the burden at the expense of the mortgagees.

But during the period of change, while prices are rising month by month, the business man has a further and greater source of windfall. Whether he is a merchant or a manufacturer, he will generally buy before he sells, and on at least a part of his stock he will run the risk of price changes. If therefore, month after month his stock appreciates on his hands, he is always selling at a better price than he expected and securing a windfall profit upon which he had not calculated. In such a period the business of trade becomes unduly easy. Any one who can borrow money

---

[1] In the article at this point Keynes adds the words 'prices rise and, which is the same thing,'.

and is not exceptionally unlucky must make a profit, which he may have done little to deserve. The continuous enjoyment of such profits engenders an expectation of their renewal. The practice of borrowing from banks is extended beyond what is normal.[1] If the market expects prices to rise still further, it is natural that stocks of commodities should be held speculatively for the rise, and for a time the mere expectation of a rise is sufficient, by inducing speculative purchases, to produce one.

Take, for example,[2] the *Statist* index number for raw materials month by month from April 1919 to March 1920:

April 1919	100	October	127
May	108	November	131
June	112	December	135
July	117	January 1920	142
August	120	February	150
September	121	March	146

It follows from this table that a man, who borrowed money from his banker and used the proceeds to purchase raw materials selected at random, stood to make a profit in every single month of this period with the exception of the last, and would have cleared 46 per cent on the average of the year. Yet bankers were not charging at this time above 7 per cent for their advances, leaving a clear profit of between 30 and 40 per cent per annum, without the exercise of any particular skill, to any person lucky enough to have embarked on these courses.[3] How much more were the opportunities of persons whose business position and expert knowledge enabled them to exercise intelligent anticipation as to the probable course of prices of particular commodities! Yet any dealer in or user of raw materials on a large scale who knew his trade was thus situated. The profits of certain kinds of business to the man who has a little skill or some luck are certain in such a period to be inordinate. Great fortunes may be made in

---

[1] The word 'normal' in the text replaces the word 'usual' in the article.

[2] In the article, the paragraph down to this point reads as follows: 'The fact that rising prices stimulate speculation, and hence the demand for loans from the banks, is well enough known, and yet perhaps the full arithmetical force of it is not sufficiently appreciated. Let us take'.

[3] The words 'these courses' in the text replace the words 'this sinful career' in the article.

a few months. But apart from all such, the steady-going business man, who would be pained and insulted at the thought of being designated speculator or profiteer, may find windfall profits dropping into his lap which he has neither sought nor desired.

Economists draw an instructive distinction between what are termed the 'money' rate of interest and the 'real' rate of interest. If a sum of money worth 100 in terms of commodities at the time when the loan is made is lent for a year at 5 per cent interest, and is only worth 90 in terms of commodities at the end of the year, the lender receives back, including his interest, what is only worth 94½. This is expressed by saying that while the *money* rate of interest was 5 per cent, the *real* rate of interest had actually been negative and equal to *minus* 5½ per cent. In the same way,[1] if at the end of the period the value of money had risen and the capital sum lent had come to be worth 110 in terms of commodities, while the *money* rate of interest would still be 5 per cent the *real* rate of interest would have been 15½ per cent.

Such considerations, even though they are not explicitly present[2] to the minds of the business world, are far from being academic. The business world may speak, and even think,[3] as though the money rate of interest could be considered by itself, without reference to the real rate. But it does not act so. The merchant or manufacturer, who is calculating whether a 7 per cent bank rate is so onerous as to compel him to curtail his operations,[4] is very much influenced by his anticipations about the prospective price of the commodity in which he is interested.

Thus, when prices are rising, the business man who borrows money is able to repay the lender with what, in terms of real value, not only represents no interest, but is even less than the

[1] The words 'in the same way' in the text replace the word 'similarly' in the article.
[2] The words 'explicitly present' in the text replace the words 'often present explicitly' in the article.
[3] In the article the verbs here are active rather than permissive.
[4] The rest of the sentence in the text replaces the following words in the article: 'takes more account, implicitly or explicitly, of the prospective course of prices of the commodity in which he is interested than of any other factor'.

capital originally advanced; that is, the real rate of interest falls to a negative value, and the borrower reaps a corresponding benefit. It is true that, in so far as a rise of prices is foreseen, attempts to get advantage from this by increased borrowing force the money rates of interest to move upwards. It is for this reason, amongst others, that a high bank rate should be associated with a period of rising prices, and a low bank rate with a period of falling prices.[1] The apparent abnormality of the money rate of interest at such times is merely the other side of the attempt of the real rate of interest to steady itself. Nevertheless[2] in a period of rapidly changing prices, the money rate of interest seldom adjusts itself adequately or fast enough to prevent the real rate from becoming abnormal. For it is not the *fact* of a given rise of prices, but the *expectation* of a rise compounded of the various possible price movements and the estimated probability of each, which affects money rates; and in countries where the currency has not collapsed completely, there has seldom or never existed a sufficient general confidence in a further rise or fall of prices to cause the short-money rate of interest to rise above 10 per cent per annum, or to fall below 1 per cent.[3] A fluctuation of this order is not sufficient to balance a movement of prices, up or down, of more than (say) 5 per cent per annum—a rate which the actual price movement has frequently exceeded.

[1] The three previous sentences in the text do not appear in the article and replace the following sentence in the article: 'It is for this reason, amongst others, that a high bank rate is, and must be, associated with a period of rising prices, and a low bank rate with a period of falling prices'.

[2] The rest of this paragraph in the text replaces the following sentences in the article:
'It is true that in a period of rapidly changing prices it is impossible for the money rate of interest, which is affected by other influences also, to adjust itself adequately or fast enough to prevent the real rate of interest from becoming abnormal. But even in such times a rise or fall (as the case may be) in the money rate of interest may nevertheless exercise a decisive influence on speculative movements, inasmuch as the merchant, who borrows money in order to take advantage of a prospective high real rate of interest, has to act in advance of the rise in prices and is calculating on a probability, not upon a certainty, with the result that he will be deterred by a movement in the money rate of interest of much less magnitude than the contrary movement in the real rate of interest, upon which indeed he is reckoning, yet is not reckoning with certainty.'

[3] The footnote Keynes used here contained the words beginning 'the merchant' in the last sentence of the above note. In his working copy he later corrected line 7, changing 'high' to 'low'.

THE POWER THAT PULLS THE STRINGS.

Will Dyson

Courtesy of I.P.C. Newspapers

Germany[1] has recently provided an illustration of the extraordinary degree in which the money rate of interest can rise in its endeavour to keep up with the real rate, when prices have continued to rise for so long and with such violence that, rightly or wrongly, every one believes that they will continue to rise further. Yet even there the money rate of interest has never risen high enough to keep pace with the rise of prices. In the autumn of 1922, the full effects were just becoming visible of the long preceding period during which the real rate of interest in Germany had reached a high negative figure, that is to say during which any one who could borrow marks and turn them into assets would have found at the end of any given period that the appreciation in the mark-value of the assets was far greater than the interest he had to pay for borrowing them. By this means great fortunes were snatched out of general calamity; and those made most who had seen first, that the right game was to borrow and to borrow and to borrow, and thus secure the difference between the real rate of interest and the money rate. But after this had been good business for many months, every one began to take a hand, with belated results on the money rate of interest. At that time, with a nominal Reichsbank rate of 8 per cent, the effective gilt-edged rate for short loans had risen to 22 per cent per annum. During the first half of 1923, the rate of the Reichsbank itself rose to 24 per cent, and subsequently to 30, and

---

[1] The next three paragraphs are peculiar to the text and replace the following paragraph in the article:

'There is, however, yet another kind of advantage from which the business man profits when prices rise: his factory, his buildings, and his plant have cost him much less than the present cost of replacing them, and this may afford him a considerable protection against the establishment of new rivals. For he will probably be prepared, at least temporarily, to meet competition by sharing with the consumer of his product some part of his windfall and can afford to lower prices, without causing himself financial embarrassment, to a level at which a newcomer could not earn normal profits. But apart from this, a newcomer will be deterred by the instability of prices and by a fear that the high level lately established may not, after all, be lasting. It will not be worth his while to incur permanent expenditure on a scale which he can only recoup if prices continue high for a long time. The natural mind is disposed after any considerable movement to anticipate a reaction and a swing backwards to what it has been habituated to think normal. All these fears and expectations, well and ill founded alike, tend to strengthen the position of the existing and established concern.'

finally 108 per cent, whilst the market rate fluctuated violently at preposterous figures, reaching at times 3 per cent *per week* for certain types of loan. With the final currency collapse of July–September 1923, the open market rate was altogether demoralised, and reached figures of 100 per cent per month. In face, however, of the rate of currency depreciation, even such figures were inadequate, and the bold borrower was still making money.

In Hungary, Poland, and Russia—wherever prices were expected to collapse yet further—the same phenomenon was present, exhibiting as through a microscope what takes place everywhere when prices are expected to rise.

On the other hand, when prices are falling 30 to 40 per cent between the average of one year and that of the next, as they were in Great Britain and in the United States during 1921, even a bank rate of 1 per cent would have been oppressive to business, since it would have corresponded to a very high rate of real interest. Any one who could have foreseen the movement even partially would have done well for himself by selling out his assets and staying out of business for the time being.

But if the depreciation of money is a source of gain to the business man, it is also the[1] occasion[2] of opprobrium.[3] To the consumer the business man's exceptional profits appear as the cause (instead of the consequence) of the hated rise of prices. Amidst the rapid fluctuations of his fortunes he himself loses his conservative instincts, and begins to think more of the large[4] gains of the moment than of the lesser, but permanent, profits of normal business. The welfare of his enterprise in the relatively distant future weighs less with him than before, and thoughts are excited[5] of a quick fortune and clearing out. His excessive gains have come to him unsought and without fault or design on his part, but once acquired he does not lightly surrender them, and

[1] The words 'also the' in the text replace the word 'an' in the article.
[2] In the article the words 'not less' appear at this point.
[3] In the article, the following additional sentence appeared at this point: 'He is unusually exposed to attack, yet deprived of his normal defences.'
[4] The word 'large' in the text replaces the word 'enormous' in the article.
[5] The word 'excited' in the text replaces the words 'not absent' in the article.

will struggle to retain his booty. With such impulses and so placed, the business man[1] is himself[2] not free from a suppressed uneasiness.[3] In his heart he loses his former self-confidence in his relation to society, in his utility and necessity in the economic scheme. He fears the future of his business and his class, and the less secure he feels his fortune to be the tighter he clings to it.[4] The business man, the prop of society and the builder of the future, to[5] whose activities and rewards there had been accorded, not long ago,[6] an almost religious sanction, he of all men and classes most respectable, praiseworthy and necessary, with whom interference was not only disastrous but almost impious, was now to suffer sidelong glances, to feel himself suspected and attacked, the victim of unjust and injurious laws—to become, and know himself half-guilty, a profiteer.

No man of spirit[7] will consent to remain poor if he believes his betters to have gained their goods by[8] lucky gambling. To convert the business man into the profiteer is to strike a blow at capitalism, because it destroys the psychological equilibrium which permits the perpetuance of unequal rewards. The economic[9] doctrine of normal profits, vaguely[10] apprehended by everyone,[11] is a necessary condition for the[12] justification of capitalism. The business man is only tolerable so long as his gains can be held to bear some relation to what, roughly and in some sense, his activities have contributed to society.

[1] In the article, the following additional words appear at this point: 'a creature of instinct and of nature, primitive in his self-expression, unsophisticated in self-knowledge'.

[2] The word 'himself' in the text replaces the word 'yet' in the article.

[3] In the article, the following additional words appear at this point: 'and a half-felt shame'.

[4] In the article, the following additional sentence appears at this point: 'With these feelings and anxieties he is the natural victim of intimidation, and shivers at a word'.

[5] The word 'to' in the text replaces the word 'over' in the article.

[6] The words 'not long ago' in the text replace the word 'lately' in the article, where this word preceded the word 'accorded'.

[7] The words of 'spirit' in the text replace the words 'who is not helpless' in the article.

[8] In the article the words 'loot or' appear at this point.

[9] The word 'economic' in the text replaces the following words in the article which followed the word profits 'of the economic text books'.

[10] The word 'vaguely' in the text replaces the word 'crudely' in the article.

[11] The word 'everyone' in the text replaces the words 'the whole community' in the article.

[12] The words 'a necessary condition for the' in the text replace the words 'the basic' in the article.

This, then, is the second disturbance to the existing economic order for which the depreciation of money is responsible. If the fall in the value of money discourages investment, it also discredits enterprise.

Not that the business man was allowed, even during the period of boom, to retain the whole of his exceptional profits. A host of popular remedies vainly attempted to cure the evils of the day; which remedies themselves—subsidies, price and rent fixing, profiteer hunting, and excess profits duties—eventually became not the least part of the evils.

In due course came the depression, with falling prices, which operate on those who hold stocks in a manner exactly opposite to rising prices. Excessive losses, bearing no relation to the efficiency of the business, took the place of windfall gains; and the effort of every one to hold as small stocks as possible brought industry to a standstill, just as previously their efforts to accumulate stocks had over-stimulated it.[1] Unemployment succeeded profiteering as the problem of the hour. But whilst the cyclical movement of trade and credit has, in the good-currency countries, partly reversed, for the time being at least, the great rise of 1920, it has, in the countries of continuing inflation, made no more than a ripple on the rapids of depreciation.

3. *The earner*

It has been[2] a[3] commonplace of economic text-books that wages tend to lag behind prices, with the result that[4] the real earnings

---

[1] The remaining sentences in this section in the text replace the following sentences in the article: 'But this cyclical movement of trade, although it accentuated the change in the value of money in 1920 and is temporarily moderating it now, is not the occasion or the subject of the present discussion. Indeed, in the countries of most serious inflation, this cyclical movement has made no more than a ripple on the rapids of depreciation. The boom exaggerated the fall in the value of money; but even in England there is no prospect of real recovery in the value of fixed incomes, and in most of continental Europe the deterioration continues.'

[2] The words 'has been' in the text replace the word 'is' in the article.

[3] The word 'a' in the text replaces the words 'an orthodox' in the article.

[4] The words 'with the result that' in the text replace the words 'and that consequently' in the article.

of the wage earner are[1] diminished during a period of rising prices. This has often been true in the past, and may be true even now of certain classes of labour which are ill-placed or ill-organised for improving their position. But in Great Britain, at any rate, and in the United States also,[2] some[3] important sections[4] of labour were able to take advantage of the situation not only to obtain money wages equivalent in purchasing power to what they had before, but to secure a real improvement, to combine this with a diminution in their hours of work (and, so far, of the work done), and to accomplish this (in the case of Great Britain)[5] at a time when the total wealth of the community as a whole had suffered a decrease. This reversal of the usual course has not been due to an accident and is traceable to definite causes.

The organisation of certain classes of labour—railwaymen, miners, dockers, and others—for the purpose of securing wage increases is better than it was. Life in the army, perhaps for the first time in the history of wars, raised in many respects the conventional standard of requirements—the soldier was better clothed, better shod, and often better fed than the labourer, and his wife, adding in wartime a separation allowance to new opportunities to earn, had also enlarged her ideas.[6]

But these influences, while they would have supplied the motive, might have lacked the means to the result if it had not been for another factor—the windfalls of the profiteer. The fact that the business man had been gaining, and gaining notoriously, considerable windfall profits in excess of the normal profits of

---

[1] At this point in the article the additional words 'at least temporarily' appear.
[2] The words 'and in the United States also' do not appear in the article.
[3] At this point in the article the additional words 'of the most' appear.
[4] The word 'sections' in the text replaces the word 'categories' in the article.
[5] The material enclosed in parentheses does not appear in the article.
[6] In the article this paragraph continues: 'And the fact that in war the necessity of maintaining what was politely termed the "morale" of the civilian had been held to excuse measures which were sometimes little better than bribery to particular sections of the community developed a habit in Government which was not discarded in peace, and the necessity of defeating the Opposition was felt to justify almost the same splendid sacrifices to the expediencies of the moment as had that of defeating the enemy.'

trade, laid him open to pressure, not only from his employees but from public opinion generally; and enabled him to meet this pressure without financial difficulty. In fact, it was worth his while to pay ransom, and to share with his workmen the good fortune of the day.

Thus the working classes improved their *relative* position in the years following the war, as against all other classes except that[1] of the 'profiteers'. In some important cases they improved their absolute position—that is to say, account being taken of shorter hours, increased money wages, and higher prices, some sections of the working classes secured for themselves a higher real remuneration for each unit of effort or work done.[2] But we cannot estimate the *stability* of this state of affairs, as contrasted with its desirability, unless we know the source from which the increased reward of the working classes was drawn. Was it due to a permanent modification of the economic factors which determine the distribution of the national product between different classes? Or was it due to some temporary and exhaustible influence connected with inflation and with the resulting disturbance in the standard of value?

A violent disturbance of the standard of value obscures the true situation, and for a time one class can benefit at the expense of another surreptitiously and without producing immediately the inevitable reaction. In such conditions a country can without knowing it expend in current consumption those savings which it thinks it is investing for the future; and it can even trench on existing capital or fail to make good its current depreciation. When the value of money is greatly fluctuating, the distinction between capital and income becomes confused. It is one[3] of the evils of a depreciating currency that it enables a community to live on its capital unawares. The increasing *money* value of the

---

[1] The words 'except that' in the text replace the words 'with the exception' in the article.

[2] In the article, the following additional sentence appears at this point: 'This, in itself, is a good thing.'

[3] The word 'one' in the text replaces the words 'not the least' in the article.

community's capital goods obscures temporarily a diminution in the real quantity of the stock.[1]

The period of depression has exacted its penalty from the working classes more[2] in the form of unemployment than by a lowering of real wages, and State assistance to the unemployed has greatly moderated even this penalty. Money wages have followed prices downwards. But the depression of 1921–2 did not reverse[3] or even greatly diminish the relative advantage gained by the working classes over the middle class during the previous years. In[4] 1923 British wage rates stood at an appreciably higher level above the pre-war rates than did the cost of living, if allowance is made for the shorter hours worked.

In Germany and Austria also, but in a far greater degree than in England or in France, the change in the value of money has thrown the burden of hard circumstances on the middle class, and hitherto the labouring class have by no means supported their full proportionate share. If it be true that university professors in Germany have some responsibility for the atmosphere

[1] In the article, this paragraph continues: 'What is taken from the investor or from savings, becoming a windfall to the business man, is only partly saved by him, being partly expended, partly paid over to the government, and partly shared with labour.'

[2] The word 'more' in the text replaces the word 'rather' in the article.

[3] The words 'did not reverse' in the text replace the words 'has not reversed' in the article. Similarly 'diminish' in the text replaces 'diminished' in the article.

[4] At this point the text and the article finally diverge. The article concludes this paragraph and comes to a close as follows:

'Even in Germany the change in the value of money has thrown on the middle classes the greatest portion of the burden of hard circumstances, and so far the labouring class have by no means supported their full share of it. If it be true that university professors in Germany have some responsibility for the atmosphere which bred war, their class has paid the penalty.

I lament the impoverishment of the middle class, out of which most good things have sprung. The consequences may slowly accumulate in a decay of knowledge and art.

But the above discussion suggests that the diminution in the production of wealth which has taken place in Europe since the war has been, to a considerable extent, at the expense, not of the consumption of any class, but at the expense of the accumulation of capital. Yet a growing population requires, for the maintenance of the same standard of life, a proportionate growth of capital. The favourable conditions for saving which existed in the nineteenth century, even though we smile at them, provided this proportionate growth. The disturbance of the pre-existing balance between classes, which in its origins is largely traceable to the changes in the value of money, may have destroyed these favourable conditions.

For these profound reasons Europe is in danger of a lasting degradation of her standards, unless bold and conservative wisdom can take control.'

which bred war, their class has paid the penalty. The effects of the impoverishment, throughout Europe, of the middle class, out of which most good things have sprung, must slowly accumulate in a decay of science and art.

We conclude that inflation redistributes wealth in a manner very injurious to the investor, very beneficial to the business man, and probably, in modern industrial conditions, beneficial on the whole to the earner. Its most striking consequence is its *injustice* to those who in good faith have committed their savings to titles to money rather than to things. But injustice on such a scale has further consequences. The above discussion suggests that the diminution in the production of wealth which has taken place in Europe since the war has been, to a certain extent, at the expense, not of the consumption of any class, but of the accumulation of capital. Moreover, inflation has not only diminished the capacity of the investing class to save but has destroyed the atmosphere of confidence which is a condition of the willingness to save. Yet a growing population requires, for the maintenance of the same standard of life, a proportionate growth of capital. In Great Britain for many years to come, regardless of what the birth rate may be from now onwards (and at the present time the number of births per day is nearly double the number of deaths), upwards of 250,000 new labourers will enter the labour market annually in excess of those going out of it. To maintain this growing body of labour at the same standard of life as before, we require not merely growing markets but a growing capital equipment. In order to keep our standards from deterioration, the national capital must grow as fast as the national labour supply, which means new savings of at least £250,000,000[1] per annum at present. The favourable conditions for saving which existed in the nineteenth century, even though we smile at them, provided a proportionate growth between capital and population.

[1] [That is to say, it costs not less than £1,000 in new capital outlay to equip a working man with organisation and appliances, which will render his labour efficient, and to house and supply himself and his family. Indeed this is probably an underestimate.]

The disturbance of the pre-existing balance between classes, which in its origins is largely traceable to the changes in the value of money, may have destroyed these favourable conditions.

On the other hand deflation, as we shall see in the second section of the next chapter, is liable, in these days of huge national debts expressed in legal-tender money, to overturn the balance so far the other way in the interests of the *rentier*, that the burden of taxation becomes intolerable on the productive classes of the community.

II. CHANGES IN THE VALUE OF MONEY, AS AFFECTING PRODUCTION

If, for any reason right or wrong, the business world *expects* that prices will fall, the processes of production tend to be inhibited; and if it expects that prices will rise, they tend to be over-stimulated. A fluctuation in the measuring-rod of value does not alter in the least the wealth of the world, the needs of the world, or the productive capacity of the world. It ought not, therefore, to affect the character or the volume of what is produced. A movement of *relative* prices, that is to say of the comparative prices of different commodities, *ought* to influence the character of production, because it is an indication that various commodities are not being produced in the exactly right proportions. But this is not true of a change, as such, in the *general* price level.

The fact that the expectation of changes in the *general* price level affects the processes of production, is deeply rooted in the peculiarities of the existing economic organisation of society, partly in those described in the preceding sections of this chapter, partly in others to be mentioned in a moment. We have already seen that a change in the general level of prices, that is to say a change in the measuring-rod, which fixes the obligation of the borrowers of money (who make the decisions which set production in motion) to the lenders (who are inactive once they have lent their money), effects a redistribution of real wealth between the two groups. Furthermore, the active group can, if they fore-

FATE OF AN EXPLORER SEARCHING FOR FOREIGN MARKETS THAT CAN AFFORD TO BUY.

Courtesy of I.P.C. Newspapers

see such a change, alter their action in advance in such a way as to minimise their losses to the other group or to increase their gains from it, if and when the expected change in the value of money occurs. If they expect a fall, it may pay them, as a group, to damp production down, although such enforced idleness

31

impoverishes society as a whole. If they expect a rise, it may pay them to increase their borrowings and to swell production beyond the point where the real return is just sufficient to recompense society as a whole for the effort made. Sometimes, of course, a change in the measuring-rod, especially if it is unforeseen, may benefit one group at the expense of the other disproportionately to any influence it exerts on the volume of production; but the tendency, in so far as the active group anticipate a change, will be as I have described it.[1] This is simply to say that the intensity of production is largely governed in existing conditions by the anticipated real profit of the entrepreneur. Yet this criterion is the right one for the community as a whole only when the delicate adjustment of interests is not upset by fluctuations in the standard of value.

But there is a further reason, connected with the above but nevertheless distinct, why modern methods of production require a stable standard—a reason springing to a certain extent out of the character of the social organisation described above, but aggravated by the technical methods of present-day productive processes. With the development of international trade, involving great distances between the place of original production and the place of final consumption, and with the increased complication of the technical processes of manufacture, the amount of *risk* which attaches to the undertaking of production and the length of time through which this risk must be carried are much greater than they would be in a comparatively small self-contained community. Even in agriculture, whilst the risk to the

---

[1] [The interests of the salaried and wage-earning classes will, in so far as their salaries and wages tend to be steadier in money value than in real value, coincide with those of the inactive capitalist group. The interests of the consumer will, in so far as he can vary the distribution of his floating resources between cash and goods purchased in advance of consumption, coincide with those of the active capitalist group; and his decisions, made in his own interests, may serve to reinforce the effect of those of the latter. But that the interests of the same individual will often be those of one of the groups in one of his capacities and of the other in another of his capacities, does not save the situation or affect the argument. For his losses in one capacity depend only infinitesimally on him personally refraining from action in his other capacity. The facts, that a man is a cannibal at home and eaten abroad, do not cancel out to render him innocuous and safe.]

consumer is diminished by drawing supplies from many different sources, which average the fluctuations of the seasons, the risk to the agricultural producer is increased, since, when his crop falls below his expectations in volume, he may fail to be compensated by a higher price. This increased risk is the price which producers have to pay for the other advantages of a high degree of specialisation and for the variety of their markets and their sources of supply.

The provision of adequate facilities for the carrying of this risk at a moderate cost is one of the greatest of the problems of modern economic life, and one of those which so far have been least satisfactorily solved. The business of keeping the productive machine in continuous operation (and thereby avoiding unemployment) would be greatly simplified if this risk could be diminished or if we could devise a better means of insurance against it for the individual entrepreneur.

A considerable part of the risk arises out of fluctuations in the *relative* value of a commodity compared with that of commodities in general during the interval which must elapse between the commencement of production and the time of consumption. This part of the risk is independent of the vagaries of money, and must be tackled by methods with which we are not concerned here. But there is also a considerable risk directly arising out of instability in the value of money. During the lengthy process of production the business world is incurring outgoings in terms of *money*—paying out in money for wages and other expenses of production—in the expectation of recouping this outlay by disposing of the product for *money* at a later date. That is to say, the business world as a whole must always be in a position where it stands to gain by a rise of price and to lose by a fall of price. Whether he likes it or not, the technique of production under a régime of money contract forces the business world always to carry a big speculative position; and if it is reluctant to carry this position, the productive process must be slackened. The argument is not affected by the fact that there is

33

some degree of specialisation of function within the business world, in so far as the professional speculator comes to the assistance of the producer proper by taking over from him a part of his risk.

Now it follows from this, not merely that the *actual occurrence* of price changes profits some classes and injures others (which has been the theme of the first section of this chapter), but that a *general fear* of falling prices may inhibit the productive process altogether. For if prices are expected to fall, not enough risk-takers can be found who are willing to carry a speculative 'bull' position, and this means that entrepreneurs will be reluctant to embark on lengthy productive processes involving a money outlay long in advance of money recoupment—whence unemployment. The *fact* of falling prices injures entrepreneurs; consequently the *fear* of falling prices causes them to protect themselves by curtailing their operations; yet it is upon the aggregate of their individual estimations of the risk, and their willingness to run the risk, that the activity of production and of employment mainly depends.

There is a further aggravation of the case, in that an expectation about the course of prices tends, if it is widely held, to be cumulative in its results up to a certain point. If prices are expected to rise and the business world acts on this expectation, that very fact causes them to rise for a time and, by verifying the expectation, reinforces it; and similarly, if it expects them to fall. Thus a comparatively weak initial impetus may be adequate to produce a considerable fluctuation.

Three generations of economists have recognised that certain influences produce a progressive and continuing change in the value of money, that others produce in it an oscillatory movement, and that the latter act cumulatively in their initial stages but produce the conditions for a reaction after a certain point. But their investigations into the oscillatory movements have been chiefly confined, until lately, to the question what kind of cause is responsible for the initial impetus. Some have been fascinated

34

by the idea that the initial cause is always the same and is astronomically regular in the times of its appearance. Others have maintained, more plausibly, that sometimes one thing operates and sometimes another.

It is one of the objects of this book to urge that the best way to cure this mortal disease of individualism is to provide that there shall never exist any confident expectation either that prices generally are going to fall or that they are going to rise; and also that there shall be no serious risk that a movement, if it does occur, will be a big one. If, unexpectedly and accidentally, a moderate movement were to occur, wealth, though it might be redistributed, would not be diminished thereby.

To procure this result by removing all possible influences towards an initial movement, whether such influences are to be found in the skies only or everywhere, would seem to be a hopeless enterprise. The remedy would lie, rather, in so controlling the standard of value that, whenever something occurred which, left to itself, would create an expectation of a change in the general level of prices, the controlling authority should take steps to counteract this expectation by setting in motion some factor of a contrary tendency. Even if such a policy were not wholly successful, either in counteracting expectations or in avoiding actual movements, it would be an improvement on the policy of sitting quietly by, whilst a standard of value, governed by chance causes and deliberately removed from central control, produces expectations which paralyse or intoxicate the government of production.

We see, therefore, that rising prices and falling prices each have their characteristic disadvantage. The inflation which causes the former means injustice to individuals and to classes, particularly to investors; and is therefore unfavourable to saving. The deflation which causes falling prices means impoverishment to labour and to enterprise by leading entrepreneurs to restrict production, in their endeavour to avoid loss to themselves; and is therefore disastrous to employment. The counterparts are, of course, also true—namely that deflation means injustice to borrowers, and that inflation leads to the overstimulation of industrial activity. But these results are not so marked as those emphasised above, because borrowers are in a better position to protect themselves from the worst effects of deflation than lenders are to protect themselves from those of inflation, and because labour is in a better position to protect itself from over-exertion in good times than from under-employment in bad times.

Thus inflation is unjust and deflation is inexpedient. Of the two perhaps deflation is, if we rule out exaggerated inflations such as that of Germany, the worse; because it is worse, in an impoverished world, to provoke unemployment than to disappoint the *rentier*. But it is not necessary that we should weigh one evil against the other. It is easier to agree that both are evils to be shunned. The individualistic capitalism of today, precisely because it entrusts saving to the individual investor and production to the individual employer, *presumes* a stable measuring-rod of value, and cannot be efficient—perhaps cannot survive—without one.

For these grave causes we must free ourselves from the deep distrust which exists against allowing the regulation of the standard of value to be the subject of *deliberate decision*. We can no longer afford to leave it in the category of which the distinguishing characteristics are possessed in different degrees by the weather, the birth rate, and the Constitution—matters which are settled by natural causes, or are the resultant of the separate action of many individuals acting independently, or require a revolution to change them.

Chapter 2

PUBLIC FINANCE AND CHANGES IN THE VALUE OF MONEY

1. *Inflation as a method of taxation*[1]

A government can live for a long time,[2] even the German government or the Russian government, by printing paper money. That is to say, it can by this means secure the command over[3] real resources, resources just as real as those obtained by taxation. The method is condemned,[4] but its[5] efficacy, up to a point, must be admitted. A government can live by this means when it can live by no other. It is the form of taxation which the public find hardest[6] to evade and[7] even the weakest government can enforce, when it can enforce nothing else. Of[8] this character have been the progressive and catastrophic inflations practised in Central and Eastern Europe, as distinguished from the limited and oscillatory inflations, experienced for example in Great Britain and the United States, which have been examined in the preceding chapter.[9]

The quantity theory of money states that[10] the amount of cash

---

[1] This section follows the article of the same title dated 27 July 1922 unless otherwise noted.

[2] The words 'live for a long time' in the text replace the words 'pay its way' in the article.

[3] The word 'over' in the text replaces the word 'of' in the article.

[4] The word 'condemned' in the text replaces the word 'reprobated' in the article.

[5] The remaining words in this sentence replace the words 'efficiency cannot be disputed' in the article.

[6] The previous words in this sentence replace the words 'This is the form of taxing the people which it is most difficult' in the article.

[7] In the article the word 'which' appears at this point.

[8] The remaining sentence in this paragraph is peculiar to the text.

[9] At this point the following additional paragraph appears in the article:

'It will simplify the argument if we take gold as representative of "real resources", although, of course, the value of gold in terms of commodities is itself a fluctuating one. I shall, therefore, in this article treat the value of a currency in terms of gold as a rough measure of its value in terms of "real resources" generally.'

[10] The preceding words in this sentence replace the word 'now' in the article.

which the community[1] requires, *assuming certain habits of business and of banking to be established*, and assuming also a given level and distribution of wealth, depends on the level of prices. If the[2] consumption and production of actual goods are unaltered but prices and wages are doubled, then twice as much cash as before is required to do the business. The[3] truth of this, properly explained and qualified, it is foolish to deny. The theory infers from this[4] that the *aggregate real value* of all the paper money in circulation remains more or less the same, irrespective of the *number of units* of it in circulation, provided the habits and prosperity of the people are not changed—i.e.[5] the community retains in the shape of cash the command over a more or less constant amount of real wealth, which is the same thing as to say that the total quantity of money in circulation has a more or less fixed purchasing power.[6]

Let us suppose that there are in circulation 9 million currency notes, and that they have altogether a value equivalent to 36 million gold dollars.[7] Suppose that the government prints a further 3 million notes, so that the amount of currency is now 12 million; then, in accordance with the above theory, the 12 million notes are still only equivalent to $36 million. In the first state of affairs, therefore, each note = $4, and in the second state of affairs each note = $3. Consequently the 9 million notes originally held by the public are now worth $27 million instead of $36 million, and the 3 million notes newly issued

[1] The words 'the community' in the text replace the word 'people' in the article, with consequent effects on the form of the verb.

[2] The word 'the' in the text replaces the word 'their' in the article.

[3] Prior to this point in the text, the words 'This is the crude quantity theory of money' appears in the article with the result that the word 'this' in the text becomes 'which' in the article.

[4] The words 'infers from this' in the text replace the word 'states' in the article.

[5] The remaining words in this sentence replace the following words in the article: 'the command over real resources retained by the community in the shape of cash is more or less constant, so that the *aggregate* quantity of money in circulation has a more or less fixed purchasing power'.

[6] [See also Chapter 3, section 1.]

[7] [It will simplify the argument to ignore the fact that the value of gold in terms of commodities is itself a fluctuating one, and to treat the value of a currency in terms of gold as a rough measure of its value in terms of 'real resources' generally.]

by the government are worth $9 million. Thus by the process of printing the additional notes the government has transferred from the public to itself an amount of resources equal to $9 million, just as successfully as if it had raised this sum in taxation.

On whom has the tax fallen? Clearly on the holders of the original 9 million notes, whose notes are now worth 25 per cent less than they were before. The inflation has amounted to a tax of 25 per cent on all holders of notes in proportion to their holdings. The burden of the tax is well spread, cannot be evaded, costs nothing to collect, and falls, in a rough sort of way, in proportion to the wealth of the victim. No wonder its superficial advantages have attracted Ministers of Finance.

Temporarily, the yield of the tax is even a little better for the government than by the above calculation. For the new notes can be passed off at first at[1] the same value as though there were still only 9 million notes altogether. It is only after the new notes get into circulation and people begin to spend them that they realise that the notes are worth less than before.

What is there to prevent the government from repeating this process over and over again? The reader must observe that the aggregate note issue is still worth $36 million. If, therefore, the government now prints a further 4 million notes, there will be 16 million notes altogether, which by the same argument as before are worth $2.25 each instead of $3, and by issuing the 4 million notes the government has, just as before, transferred an amount of resources equal to $9 million from the public to itself. The holders of notes have again suffered a tax of 25 per cent in proportion to their holdings.

Like other forms of taxation, these exactions, if overdone and out of proportion to the wealth of the community, must diminish its prosperity and lower its standards, so that at the lower standard of life the aggregate value of the currency may fall and still

---

[1] The previous words of this sentence replace the word sequence 'For at first it is able to pass off some of the new notes as having' in the article.

be enough to go round. But this effect cannot[1] interfere very much with the efficacy of taxing by inflation. Even if[2] the aggregate real value of the currency falls for these reasons to a half or two-thirds of what it was before, which represents a tremendous lowering of the standards of life, this only means that the quantity of notes which the government must issue in order to obtain a given result must be raised proportionately. It remains true that by this means the government can still secure for itself a large share of the available surplus of the community.

Has the public[3] in the last resort no remedy, no means of protecting itself against these ingenious depredations? It has only one remedy—to change its habits in the use of money. The[4] initial assumption on which our argument rested was that the community did *not* change its habits in the use of money.

Experience shows that the public generally is very slow to grasp the situation and embrace the remedy. Indeed, at first there may be a change of habit[5] in the wrong direction, which actually facilitates[6] the government's operations. The public is so much accustomed[7] to thinking of money as the ultimate standard, that, when prices begin to rise, believing that the rise must be temporary,[8] they tend to hoard their money and to postpone purchases, with the result that they hold in monetary form a *larger* aggregate of real value than before. And, similarly, when

[1] The previous words of this sentence replace the words 'But even this does not' in the article.

[2] At this point in the article the words 'for the above reasons' appear, rather than later in the sentence as in the text.

[3] The previous words in this sentence are replaced in the article by the following: 'So far the position, from the point of view of the public, seems quite desperate. Have they'. The change to 'they' from 'it' results in certain grammatical changes in the next sentence of the text from the article.

[4] This sentence in the text replaces the following sentence in the article: 'This was the initial assumption on which our argument rested—that the habits of the community in the use of money remain unchanged.'

[5] The preceding words in this sentence replace the words 'Indeed, at first such change of habit as there is may be' in the article.

[6] The words 'which actually facilitates' in the text replace the words 'and may actually facilitate' in the article.

[7] The words 'much accustomed' in the text replace the word 'habituated' in the article.

[8] In the article the material enclosed by the commas in the text follows the words 'they tend'.

the fall in the real value of the money is reflected in the exchanges, foreigners, thinking that the fall is abnormal and temporary, purchase the money for the purpose of hoarding it.

But sooner or later the second phase sets in. The public discover[1] that it is the holders of notes who suffer taxation and defray the expenses of government, and they begin to change their habits and to economise in their holding of notes. They can do this in various ways: (1) instead of keeping some part of their ultimate reserves in money they can spend this money on durable objects, jewellery or household goods, and keep their reserves in this form instead; (2) they can reduce the amount of till money and pocket money that they keep[2] and the average length of time for which they keep it,[3] even at the cost[4] of great personal inconvenience; and (3)[5] they can employ foreign money in many transactions where it would have been more natural and convenient to use their own.

By these means they can get along and do their business with an amount of notes having an aggregate real value substantially[6] less than before. For example, the notes in circulation become worth altogether $20 million instead of $36 million, with the result that the next inflationary levy by the government, falling on a smaller amount, must be at a greater rate in order to yield a given sum.

[1] In the article, the words 'in effect' are added at this point.
[2] In the text the remaining words before the comma do not appear in the article.
[3] [In Moscow the unwillingness to hold money except for the shortest possible time reached at one period a fantastic intensity. If a grocer sold a pound of cheese, he ran off with the roubles as fast as his legs could carry him to the Central Market to replenish his stocks by changing them into cheese again, lest they lost their value before he got there; thus justifying the prevision of economists in naming the phenomenon 'velocity of circulation'! In Vienna, during the period of collapse, mushroom exchange banks sprang up at every street corner, where you could change your krone into Zurich francs within a few minutes of receiving them, and so avoid the risk of loss during the time it would take you to reach your usual bank. It became a seasonable witticism to allege that a prudent man at a café ordering a bock of beer should order a second bock at the same time, even at the expense of drinking it tepid, lest the price should rise meanwhile.] This footnote originally appeared as a paragraph somewhat later in the article.
[4] The word 'cost' in the text replaces the word 'expense' in the article.
[5] At this point in the article the words 'in the last resort' appear.
[6] The word 'substantially' does not appear in the article.

When[1] the public take alarm faster than they can change their habits, and, in their efforts to avoid loss, run down the amount of real resources, which they hold in the form of money, *below* the working minimum, seeking to supply their daily needs for cash by borrowing, they get penalised, as in Germany in 1923, by prodigious rates of money interest. The rates rise, as we have seen in the previous chapter, until the rate of interest on money equals or exceeds the anticipated rate of depreciation of money. Indeed, it is always likely, when money is rapidly depreciating, that there will be recurrent periods of scarcity of currency, because the public, in their anxiety not to hold too much money, will fail to provide themselves even with the minimum which they will require in practice.

Whilst economists have sometimes described these phenomena in terms of an increase in the velocity of circulation due to loss of confidence in the currency; nevertheless there are not, I think, many passages in economic literature where the matter is clearly analysed. Professor Cannan's article on 'The Application of the Apparatus of Supply and Demand to Units of Currency' (*Economic Journal*, December 1921) is one of the most noteworthy. He points out that the common assumption that 'the elasticity of demand for money is unity' is equivalent to the assertion that a mere variation in the quantity of money does not affect the willingness and habits of the public as holders of purchasing power in that form. But in extreme cases this assumption does not hold; for if it did, there would be no limit to the sums which the government could extract from the public by means of inflation. It is, therefore, unsafe to assume that the elasticity of demand is necessarily unity. Professor Lehfeldt followed this up in a subsequent issue of the *Economic Journal* (December 1922)

---

[1] At this point the article and the text diverge sharply in form. The article dealt briefly, in one paragraph, with the idea of the velocity of circulation and then went on to discuss German, Austrian and Russian conditions in 1922. The text continues discussing velocity in more detail and considering the experiences of the same three countries in the light of another year's events. Both the article and this section conclude with the same four sentences found on page 53. The remaining sections of the original article appear as Appendix I.

by a calculation of the actual elasticity of demand for money in some recent instances. He found that between July 1920 and April 1922, the elasticity of demand for money fell to an average of about 0·73 in Austria, 0·67 in Poland, and 0·5 in Germany. Thus in the last stages of inflation the prodigious increase in the velocity of circulation may have as much, or more, effect in raising prices and depreciating the exchanges than the increase in the volume of notes. The note-issuing authorities often cry out against what they regard as the unfair and anomalous fact of the notes falling in value *more* than in proportion to their increased volume. Yet it is nothing of the kind; it is merely the result of the one method to evade a crushing burden left open to the public, who discover for themselves, sooner than the financiers, that the law of unit elasticity in their demand for money can be escaped.

Nevertheless, it is evident that so long as the public use money at all, the government can continue to raise resources by inflation. Moreover, the conveniences of using money in daily life are so great that the public are prepared, rather than forgo them, to pay the inflationary tax, provided it is not raised to a prohibitive level. Like other conveniences of life the use of money is taxable, and, although for various reasons this particular form of taxation is highly inexpedient, a government can get resources by a *continuous* practice of inflation, even when this is foreseen by the public generally, unless the sums they seek to raise in this way are very grossly excessive. Just as a toll can be levied on the use of roads or a turnover tax on business transactions, so also on the use of money. The higher the toll and the tax, the less traffic on the roads, and the less business transacted, so also the less money carried. But some traffic is so indispensable, some business so profitable, some money payments so convenient, that only a very high levy will stop completely all traffic, all business, all payments. A government has to remember, however, that even if a tax is not prohibitive it may be unprofitable, and that a medium, rather than an extreme, imposition will yield the greatest gain.

5-2

Suppose that the rate of inflation is such that the value of the money falls by half every year, and suppose that the cash used by the public for retail purchases in shops is turned over 100 times a year (i.e. stays in one pocket for half a week on the average); then this is only equivalent to a turnover tax of $\frac{1}{2}$ per cent on each transaction. The public will gladly pay such a tax rather than suffer the trouble and inconvenience of barter with trams and tradesmen. Even if the value of the money falls by half every month, the public, by keeping their pocket money so low that they turn it over once a day on the average instead of only twice a week, can still keep the tax down to the equivalent of less than 2 per cent on each transaction, or more precisely $4d$ in the £. Even such a terrific rate of depreciation as this is not sufficient, therefore, to counterbalance the advantages of using money rather than barter in the trifling business of daily life. This is the explanation why, even in Germany and in Russia, the government's notes remained current for many retail transactions.

For certain other purposes, however, to which money is put in a modern community, the inflationary tax becomes prohibitive at a much earlier stage. As a store of value, for example, money is rapidly discarded, as soon as further depreciation is confidently anticipated. As a unit of account, for contracts and for balance sheets, it quickly becomes worse than useless, although for such purposes the privilege of the current money as legal tender for the discharge of debts stands in the way of its being discarded as soon as it ought to be.

In the last phase, when the use of the legal-tender money has been discarded for all purposes except trifling out-of-pocket expenditure, inflationary taxation has at last defeated itself. For in that case the total value of the note issue, which is sufficient to meet the public's minimum requirements, amounts to a figure relatively so trifling that the amount of resources which the government can hope to raise by yet further inflation—without pushing it to a point at which the money will be discarded even for out-of-pocket trifles—is correspondingly small. Thus at last, unless it is employed with some measure of moderation, this potent instrument of governmental exaction breaks in the hands of those that use it, and leaves them at the same time with the rest of their fiscal system in total ruins—out of which, in the ebb and flow of the economic life of nations, may emerge once more a reformed and admirable system. The chervonetz of Moscow and the krone of Vienna are already stabler units than the franc or the lira.

All these matters can be illustrated from the recent experiences of Germany, Austria, and Russia. The following tables show the gold value of the note issues of these countries at various dates.

The characteristics of each phase emerge clearly. The tables show, first of all, how quickly, during the period of collapse, the rate of the depreciation of the value of the money outstrips the

GERMANY	Volume of note issue in milliard paper marks	Number of paper marks = 1 gold mark	Value of note issue in milliard gold marks
December 1920	81	17	4·8
December 1921	122	46	2·7
March 1922	140	65	2·2
June 1922	180	90	2·0
September 1922	331	349	0·9
December 1922	1,293	1,778	0·7
February 1923	2,266	11,200	0·2
March 1923	4,956	4,950	1·0
June 1923	17,000	45,000	0·4
August 1923	116,000	1,000,000	0·116

AUSTRIA	Volume of note issue in milliard paper krone	Number of paper krone = 1 gold krone	Value of note issue in million gold krone
June 1920	17	27	620
December 1920	30	70	430
December 1921	174	533	326
March 1922	304	1,328	229
June 1922	550	2,911	189
September 1922	2,278	14,473	157
December 1922	4,080	14,473	282
March 1923	4,238	14,363	295
August 1923	5,557	14,369	387

RUSSIA	Volume of note issue in milliard paper roubles	Number of paper roubles[1] = 1 gold rouble	Value of note issue in million gold roubles
January 1919	61	103	592
January 1920	225	1,670	134
January 1921	1,169	26,000	45
January 1922	17,539	172,000	102[2]
March 1922	48,535	1,060,000	46
May 1922	145,635	3,800,000	38[3]
July 1922	320,497	4,102,000	78
October 1922	815,486	6,964,000	117
January 1923	2,138,711	15,790,000	135
June 1923	8,050,000	97,690,000	82[4]

[1] 'Gosplan' figures for 1923, Moscow Economic Institute figures previously.
[2] The increase is due to the reintroduction of the use of money in State transactions as a result of the new economic policy.
[3] Lowest point reached.
[4] The decrease may be attributed to the introduction of the chervonetz (see p. 49 below).

rate of the inflation of its volume. During the collapse of the German mark beginning with December 1920, the rate of depreciation proceeded for some time roughly twice as fast as that of the inflation, and eventually by June 1923, when the volume of the note issue had increased 200-fold compared with December 1920, the value of a paper mark had fallen 2,500-fold. The figures given above for Austria begin at a rather later stage of the débâcle. But if we equate Austria in June 1920 to Germany in December 1920, the progress of events between that date and September 1922 is roughly comparable to that in Germany between December 1920 and May 1923. The figures for Russia between January 1919 and the early part of 1923 also exhibit the same general features.

These tables all commence after a considerable depreciation had already occurred and the gold value of the aggregate note issue had fallen considerably below the normal.[1] Nevertheless their earliest entries still belong to the period when an eventual recovery was still widely anticipated and the general public had

[1] [The pre-war currency of Germany was estimated at about 6 milliard gold marks (£300 million), or nearly £5 per head.]

not at all appreciated what they were in for. They indicate that as the situation develops from this point onwards and the use of money is discarded except for retail transactions, the aggregate value of the note issue falls by about four-fifths. As the result of extreme panic or depression a further fall may occur for a time; but, unless the money is discarded altogether, a minimum is reached eventually from which the least favourable circumstance will cause a sharp recovery.

The temporary recovery in Germany after the collapse of February 1923 exhibited how a point may come when, if the money is to continue in use at all, a bottom is reached and a technical position is created in which some recovery is possible. When the gold value of the currency has fallen to a very low figure, it is easy for the government, if it has any external resources at all, to give sufficient support to prevent the exchange from falling further for the time being. And since by that time the public will have carried their attempts to economise the use of money to a pitch of inconvenience which it is impracticable to continue, even a moderate weakening in the degree of their distrust of the future value of the money will lead to some increase in their use of it; with the result that the aggregate value of the note issue will tend to recover. By February 1923 these conditions existed in Germany in a high degree. The German government was able within two months, in the face of most adverse political conditions, to double the exchange value of the mark whilst simultaneously more than doubling the note circulation. Even so the gold value of the note issue was only brought back to what it had been six months earlier; and if even a moderate degree of confidence had been restored, it might have been possible to bring the value of the note circulation of Germany up to (say) 2 milliard gold marks (£100 million) at least, which is probably about the lowest figure at which it can stand permanently, unless every one is to put himself to intolerable inconvenience in his efforts to hold as little money as possible. Incidentally the government is able during the period of

47

recovery to obtain, once more, through the issue of notes the command over a considerable amount of real resources.

In Austria, where, at the date of writing, the exchange has been stabilised for a year, the same phenomenon has been apparent with the growth of confidence, the gold value of the note issue having been raised to nearly two and a half times the low point reached in September 1922. The fact of stabilisation, with foreign aid, has by increasing confidence permitted this increase of the note issue without imperilling the stabilisation, and will probably permit in course of time a substantial further increase.

Even in Russia a sort of equilibrium seems to have been reached. There the last phase had appeared by the middle of 1922, when a tenfold inflation in six months[1] had brought the aggregate value of the note issue below £4 million, which clearly could not be adequate for the transaction of the business of Russia even in its present condition. A point had been reached when the use of paper roubles was being dispensed with altogether. At about that date I had the opportunity of discussion at Genoa with some of the Soviet financiers. They have always been more self-conscious and deliberate than others in their monetary policy. They maintained at that time that, with the help of legal compulsion to employ paper roubles for certain types of transaction, these roubles could always be maintained in circulation up to a certain *minimum* real value, however certain the public might be as to their ultimate worthlessness. According to this calculation, it would always be possible to raise (say) £3 million to £4 million per annum by this method, even though the paper rouble regularly fell in value at the rate of a tenfold or a hundredfold a year (one or more noughts being struck off the monetary unit annually for convenience of calculation). During the year following they did, in fact, decidedly better than this, and, by reducing the rate of inflation to a figure not much in

[1] [Recent experience everywhere seems to show that it is possible to inflate 100 per cent every three months without entirely killing the use of money in retail transactions, but that a greater rate of inflation than this can only be indulged in at the peril of total collapse.]

excess of 100 per cent per three months, were able to raise the aggregate value of the note issue to more than double the lowest point reached. The equivalent of something like £15 million seems to have been raised during the year (April 1922–April 1923) by this means towards the expenses of government, at the cost of having to strike only one nought off the monetary unit for the whole year![1] At the same time, in order to furnish a reliable store of value and a basis for foreign trade, the Soviet government introduced in December 1922 a new currency unit (the chervonetz, or gold ducat), freely convertible on sterling-exchange standard principles, alongside the paper rouble, which was still indispensable as an instrument of taxation. So far this new bank note has kept respectable. By August 1923 its circulation had risen to nearly 16 million having a value of about £16 million, and its exchange value had kept steady, the State Bank undertaking to convert the chervonetz on a parity with the £ sterling.[2] Thus by the middle of 1923 the aggregate value of the Russian note issues, good and bad money together, had risen to the substantial figure of £25 million, as compared with barely £4 million at the date of the Genoa Conference in May 1922, thus indicating the return of confidence and the re-inauguration of a monetary régime. Russia provides an instructive example (at least for the moment) of a sound money for substantial transactions alongside small change for daily life, the progressive depreciation on which merely represents a quite supportable rate of turnover tax.

[1] [The Soviet government have always regarded monetary inflation quite frankly as an instrument of taxation, and have themselves calculated that the purchasing power secured to the State by this means has amounted in the past to the following sums (in million gold roubles):

1918	525
1919	380
1920	186
1921	143
1922 (January to March)	58

or (say) £130 million altogether.]

[2] [So far the chervonetz has generally sold at a small premium, the rates being: 15 March 1923, ch. 1 = £1·07; 17 April 1923, ch 1 = £1·05; 15 June 1923, ch. 1 = £0·94; 27 July 1923, ch. 1 = £1·05.]

The collapse of the currency in Germany, which was the chief contributory cause to the fall to Dr Cuno's government in August 1923, was due, not so much to taxing by inflation—for that had been going on for years—as to an increase in the *rate* of inflation to a level almost prohibitive for daily transactions and quite destructive of the legal-tender money as a unit of account. We have seen that what concerns the use of money in the retail transactions of daily life is the *rate* of depreciation, rather than the absolute amount of depreciation as compared with some earlier date.

In the middle of 1922[1] I estimated, very roughly, that the German government had then been obtaining for some time past the equivalent of something between £75 million and £100 million per annum by means of printing money. Up to that time, however, a substantial proportion of these receipts had been contributed through the purchase of mark notes by speculative foreigners. Nevertheless the German public itself had probably paid upwards of £50 million per annum in this form of taxation. Since the German note issue was still worth £240 million so lately as December 1920 (see the table on p. 45) and had not fallen below £100 million even in the middle of 1922, the rate of depreciation represented by the above, whilst sufficiently disastrous to the mark as a store of value or as a unit of account, had been by no means prohibitive to its continued use in daily life. In the latter half of 1922, however, the public learnt to make enough further economies in the use of the mark as money to reduce the value of the total note issue to about £60 million. The first effect of the Ruhr occupation was, as we have seen above (p. 47), to bring down the note issue below the minimum to which the public could adjust their habits, which resulted in the temporary recovery of March 1923. Nevertheless by the middle of 1923 the public was able to get along with a note issue worth about £20 million. All this time the German government had continued to raise resources equivalent to round about £1 million

---

[1] In the original article on which this chapter was based. [Ed.] See below p. 163.

a week by note-printing—which meant a depreciation of 5 per cent a week even if the public had been unable to reduce any further the value of the aggregate note issue, and came in practice to about 10 per cent a week allowing for their yet further economies in the use of mark currency.

But the expenses of the Ruhr resistance, coupled with the complete breakdown of other sources of taxation, had led, by May and June 1923, to the government's raising the equivalent of, first, £2 million and then £3 million a week by note-printing. On a note issue, of which the total value had sunk by that time to about £20 million, this was pushing inflationary taxation to a preposterous and suicidal point. The social disorganisation, resulting from a rapid movement to do without the mark altogether, quickly resulted in Dr Cuno's fall.[1] The climax was reached when, in Dr Cuno's last days, the government doubled the note issue in a week and raised the equivalent of £3 million in that period out of a note issue worth about £4 million altogether—a performance far transcending the wildest extravagances of the Soviet.

By the time this book is published, Dr Cuno's successors may have solved, or failed to solve, the problem facing them. However this may be, the restoration of a serviceable unit of account seems to be the first step. This is a necessary preliminary to the escape of the German financial system from the vicious circle in which it now moves. The government cannot introduce a sound money, because, in the absence of other revenue, the printing of an unsound money is the only way by which it can live. Yet a serviceable unit of account is a prerequisite of the collection of

[1] [It is necessary to admit that Dr Cuno's failure to control incompetence at the Treasury and at the Reichsbank was bound to bring this about. During this catastrophic period those responsible for the financial policy of Germany did not do a single wise thing, or show the least appreacition of what was happening. The profits of note-printing were not even monopolised by the government, and Herr Havenstein continued to allow the German banks to share in them, by discounting their bills at the Reichsbank at a rate of discount far below the rate of depreciation. Only at the end of August 1923 did the Reichsbank begin to require that borrowers should make good on repayment a percentage of the loss due to the depreciation of the borrowed marks (as reckoned by the dollar exchange) during the currency of the loan.]

the normal sources of revenue. The best course, therefore, is to remain content for a little longer with an unsound money as a source of revenue, but to introduce immediately a steady unit of account (the relation of which to the unsound money could be officially fixed daily or weekly) as a preliminary to the restoration of the normal sources of revenue.

The recent history of German finance can be summarised thus. Reliance on inflationary taxation, whilst extremely productive to the exchequer in its earliest stages especially whilst the foreign speculator was still buying paper marks, gradually broke down the mark as a serviceable unit of account, one of the effects of which was to render unproductive the greater part of the rest of the revenue-collecting machinery—most taxes being necessarily assessed at some interval of time before they are collected. The failure of the rest of the revenue rendered the Treasury more and more dependent on inflation, until finally the use of legal-tender money had been so far abandoned by the public that even the inflationary tax ceased to be productive and the government was threatened by literal bankruptcy. At this stage, the fiscal organisation of the country had been so thoroughly destroyed and its social and economic organisation so grievously disordered, as in Russia eighteen months earlier, that it was a perplexing problem to devise ways and means by which the government could live during the transitional period whilst the normal machinery for collecting revenue was being re-created, especially in face of the struggle with France proceeding at the same time. Nevertheless the problem is not insoluble; many suggestions could be made; and a way out will doubtless be found at length.

It is common to speak as though, when a government pays its way by inflation, the people of the country avoid taxation. We have seen that this is not so. What is raised by printing notes is just as much taken from the public as is a beer duty or an income tax. What a government spends the public pay for. There is no such thing as an uncovered deficit. But in some countries it seems possible to please and content the public, for a time at least, by giving them, in return for the taxes they pay, finely engraved acknowledgements on watermarked paper. The income-tax receipts, which we in England receive from the Surveyor, we throw into the wastepaper basket; in Germany they call them bank notes and put them into their pocket-books; in France they are termed *rentes* and are locked up in the family safe.

2. *Currency depreciation* versus *capital levy*

We have seen in the preceding section the extent to which a government can make use of currency inflation for the purpose of securing income to meet its outgoings. But there is a second way in which inflation helps a government to make both ends meet, namely by reducing the burden of its pre-existing liabilities in so far as they have been fixed in terms of money. These liabilities consist, in the main, of the internal debt. Every step of depreciation obviously means a reduction in the real claims of the *rentes*-holders against their government.

It would be too cynical to suppose that, in order to secure the advantages discussed in this section, governments (except, possibly, the Russian government) depreciate their currencies *on purpose*. As a rule they are, or consider themselves to be, driven to it by their necessities. The requirements of the Treasury to meet sudden exceptional outgoings—for a war or to pay the consequences of defeat—are likely to be the original occasion of, at least *temporary*, inflation. But the most cogent reason for *permanent* depreciation, that is to say *devaluation*, or the policy of fixing the value of the currency permanently at the low level to which a temporary emergency has driven it, is generally to be found in the fact that a restoration of the currency to its former value would raise the recurrent annual burden of the fixed charges of the National Debt to an insupportable level.

There is, nevertheless, an alternative to devaluation in such cases, provided the opponents of devaluation are prepared to face it in time, which they generally are not—namely a capital levy. The purpose of this section is to bring out clearly the *alternative* character of these two methods of moderating the claims of the *rentier*, when the State's contractual liabilities, fixed in terms of money, have reached an excessive proportion of the national income.

The active and working elements in no community, ancient or modern, will consent to hand over to the *rentier* or bond-holding class more than a certain proportion of the fruits of their work. When the piled-up debt demands more than a tolerable proportion, relief has usually been sought in one or other of two out of the three possible methods. The first is repudiation. But, except as the accompaniment of revolution, this method is too crude, too deliberate, and too obvious in its incidence. The victims are immediately aware and cry out too loud; so that, in the absence of revolution, this solution may be ruled out at present, as regards *internal* debt, in Western Europe.

The second method is currency depreciation, which becomes devaluation when it is fixed and confirmed by law. In the countries of Europe lately belligerent, this expedient has been adopted already on a scale which reduces the real burden of the debt by from 50 to 100 per cent. In Germany the National Debt has been by these means practically obliterated, and the bond-holders have lost everything. In France the real burden of the debt is less than a third of what it would be if the franc stood at par; and in Italy only a quarter. The owners of small savings suffer quietly, as experience shows, these enormous depredations, when they would have thrown down a government which had taken from them a fraction of the amount by more deliberate but juster instruments.

This fact, however, can scarcely justify such an expedient on its merits. Its indirect evils are many. Instead of dividing the burden between all classes of wealth-owners according to a graduated scale, it throws the whole burden on to the owners of fixed-interest bearing stocks, lets off the entrepreneur capitalist and even enriches him, and hits small savings equally with great fortunes. It follows the line of least resistance, and responsibility cannot be brought home to individuals. It is, so to speak, nature's remedy, which comes into silent operation when the body politic has shrunk from curing itself.

The remaining, the scientific, expedient, the capital levy, has never yet been tried on a large scale; and perhaps it never will be. It is the rational, the deliberate method. But it is difficult to explain, and it provokes violent prejudice by coming into conflict with the deep instincts by which the love of money protects itself. Unless the patient understands and approves its purpose, he will not submit to so severe a surgical operation.

Once currency depreciation has done its work, I should not advocate the unwise, and probably impracticable, policy of retracing the path with the aid of a capital levy. But if it has become clear that the claims of the bond-holder are more than the taxpayer can support, and if there is still time to choose between the policies of a levy and of further depreciation, the levy must surely be preferred on grounds both of expediency and of justice. It is an overwhelming objection to the method of currency depreciation, as compared with that of the levy, that it falls entirely upon persons whose wealth is in the form of claims to legal-tender money, and that these are generally, amongst the capitalists, the poorer capitalists. It is entirely ungraduated; it falls on small savings just as hardly as on big ones; and incidentally it benefits the capitalist entrepreneur class for the reasons explained in chapter 1. Unfortunately the small savers who have most to lose by currency depreciation are precisely the sort of conservative people who are most alarmed by a capital levy; whilst, on the other hand, the entrepreneur class must obviously prefer depreciation which does not hit them very much and may actually enrich them. It is the combination of these two forces which will generally bring it about that a country will prefer the inequitable and disastrous courses of currency depreciation to the scientific deliberation of a levy.

There is a respectable and influential body of opinion which, repudiating with vehemence the adoption of either expedient, fulminates alike against devaluations and levies, on the ground that they infringe the untouchable sacredness of contract; or rather of vested interest, for an alteration of the legal tender and the imposition of a tax on property are neither of them in the least illegal or even contrary to precedent. Yet such persons, by overlooking one of the greatest of all social principles, namely the fundamental distinction between the right of the individual to repudiate contract and the right of the State to control vested interest, are the worst enemies of what they seek to preserve. For nothing can preserve the integrity of contract between individuals, except a discretionary authority in the State to revise what has become intolerable. The powers of uninterrupted usury are too great. If the accretions of vested interest were to grow without mitigation for many generations, half the population would be no better than slaves to the other half. Nor can the fact that in time of war it is easier for the State to borrow than to tax, be allowed permanently to enslave the taxpayer to the bondholder. Those who insist that in these matters the State is in exactly the same position as the individual will, if they have their way, render impossible the continuance of an individualist society, which depends for its existence on moderation.

These conclusions might be deemed obvious if experience did not show that many conservative bankers regard it as more consonant with their cloth, and also as economising thought, to shift public discussion of financial topics off the logical on to an alleged 'moral' plane, which means a realm of thought where vested interest can be triumphant over the common good without further debate. But it makes them untrustworthy guides in a perilous age of transition. The State must never neglect the importance of so acting in ordinary matters as to promote certainty and security in business. But when great decisions are to be made, the State is a sovereign body of which the purpose is to promote the greatest good of the whole. When, therefore, we enter the realm of State action, *everything* is to be considered and weighed on its merits. Changes in death duties, income tax, land tenure, licensing, game laws, church establishment, feudal rights, slavery, and so on through all ages, have received the same denunciations from the absolutists of contract, who are the real parents of revolution.

In our own country the question of the capital levy depends for its answer on whether the great increase in the claims of the bond-holder, arising out of the fact that it was easier, and perhaps more expedient, to raise a large part of the current costs of the war by loans rather than by taxes, is more than the taxpayer can be required, in the long run, to support. The high levels of the death duties and of the income and super taxes on unearned income, by which the net return to the bond-holder is substantially diminished,[1] modify the case. Nevertheless, immediately after the war, when it seemed that the normal budget could scarcely be balanced without a level of taxation of which a tax on earned income at a standard rate between 6s and 10s in the £ would be typical, a levy seemed to be necessary. At the present time the case is rather more doubtful. It is not yet possible to know how the normal budget will work out, and much depends on the level at which sterling prices are stabilised. If the level of sterling prices is materially lowered, whether in pursuance of a policy of restoring the old gold parity or for any other reason, a levy may be required. If, however, sterling prices are stabilised somewhere between 80 and 100 per cent above the pre-war level—a settlement probably desirable on other grounds—and if the progressive prosperity of the country is restored, then perhaps we may balance our future budgets without oppressive taxation on earned income and without a levy either. A levy is from the practical view perfectly feasible, and is not open to more objection than any other *new* tax of like magnitude. Nevertheless, like all new taxes, it cannot be brought in without friction, and is,

---

[1] The net return to the French *rentier* is more than 6 per cent; to the British not much above 3 per cent.

therefore, scarcely worth advocating for its own sake merely in substitution for an existing tax of similar incidence. It is to be regarded as the fairest and most expedient method of adjusting the burden of taxation between past accumulations and the fruits of present efforts, whenever, in the general judgment of the country, the discouragement to the latter is excessive. A levy is to be judged, not by itself, but as against the practicable alternatives. Experience shows with great certainty that the active part of the community will not submit in the long run to pay too much to vested interest, and, if the necessary adjustment is not made in one way, it will be made in another—probably by the depreciation of the currency.

In several countries the existing burden of the internal debt renders devaluation inevitable and certain sooner or later. It will be sufficient to illustrate the case by reference to the situation of France—the home of absolutism of all kinds, and hence, sooner or later, of *bouleversement*. The finances of Humpty Dumpty are as follows:

At the end of 1922 the internal debt of France, excluding altogether her external debt, exceeded 250 milliard francs. Further borrowing budgeted for in the ensuing period, together with loans on reconstruction account guaranteed by the government, may bring this total to the neighbourhood of 300 milliards by the end of 1923. The service of this debt will absorb nearly 18 milliards per annum. The total normal receipts under the provisional[1] budget for 1923 are estimated at around 23 milliards. That is to say, the service of the debt will shortly absorb, at the value of the franc current early in 1923, almost the entire yield of taxation. Since other government expenditure in the ordinary budget (i.e. excluding war pensions and future expenditure on reconstruction) cannot be put below 12 milliards a year, it

---

[1] The forecasts of the final outcome of the year are frequently changed and may be somewhat different from the above, though not sufficiently to affect the argument. M. de Lasteyrie has lately pointed out with pride how the further depreciation of the franc, since he first introduced his budget, is already improving the receipts measured in terms of francs.

follows that, even on the improbable hypothesis that further expenditure in the extraordinary budget after 1923 will be paid for by Germany, the yield of taxation must be increased permanently by 30 per cent to make both ends meet. If, however, the franc were to depreciate to (say) 100 to the pound sterling, the ordinary budget could be balanced by taking little more of the real income of the country than in 1922.

In these circumstances it will be difficult, if not impossible, to avoid the subtle assistance of a further depreciation. What, then, is to be said of those who still discuss seriously the project of restoring the franc to its former parity? In such an event the already intolerable burden of the *rentier*'s claims would be about trebled. It is unthinkable that the French taxpayer would submit. Even if the franc were put back to par by a miracle, it could not stay there. Fresh inflation due to the inadequacy of tax receipts must drive it anew on its downward course. Yet I have assumed the cancellation of the whole of France's external debt, and the assumption by Germany of the burdens of the extraordinary budget after 1923, an assumption which is not justified by present expectations. These facts alone render it certain that the franc cannot be restored to its former value.

France must come in due course to some compromise between increasing taxation, and diminishing expenditure, and reducing what they owe their *rentiers*. I have not much doubt that the French public, as they have hitherto, will consider a further dose of depreciation—attributing it to the 'bad will' of Germany or to financial Machiavellism in London and New York—as far more conservative, orthodox, and in the interest of small savers, than a justly constructed capital levy, the odium of which could be less easily escaped by the French Ministry of Finance.

If we look ahead, averting our eyes from the ups and downs which can make and unmake fortunes in the meantime, the level of the franc is going to be settled in the long run not by speculation or the balance of trade, or even the outcome of the Ruhr adventure, but by the proportion of his earned income which the French taxpayer will permit to be taken from him to pay the claims of the French *rentier*. The level of the franc exchange will continue to fall until the commodity value of the francs due to the *rentier* has fallen to a proportion of the national income which accords with the habits and mentality of the country.

Chapter 3

THE THEORY OF MONEY AND OF THE FOREIGN EXCHANGES

The evil consequences of instability in the standard of value have now been sufficiently described. In this chapter[1] we must lay the theoretical foundations for the practical suggestions of the concluding chapters. Most academic treatises on monetary theory have been based, until lately, on so firm a presumption of a gold standard régime that they need to be adapted to the existing régime of mutually inconvertible paper standards.

1. *The quantity theory of money*

This theory is fundamental. Its correspondence with fact is not open to question.[2] Nevertheless it is often misstated and misrepresented. Goschen's saying of sixty years ago, that 'there are many persons who cannot hear the relation of the level of prices to the volume of currency affirmed without a feeling akin to irritation', still holds good.

The theory flows from the fact that money as such has no utility except what is derived from its exchange value, that is to say from the utility of the things which it can buy. Valuable articles other than money have a utility in themselves. Provided that they are divisible and transferable, the total amount of this utility increases with their quantity—it will not increase in full proportion to the quantity, but, up to the point of satiety, it does increase.

---

[1] Parts of this chapter raise, unavoidably, matters of much greater difficulty to the layman than the rest of the book. The reader whose interest in the theoretical foundations is secondary can pass on.

[2] 'The quantity theory is often defended and opposed as though it were a definite set of propositions that must be either true or false. But in fact the formulae employed in the exposition of that theory are merely devices for enabling us to bring together in an orderly way the principal causes by which the value of money is determined' (Pigou).

If an article is used for money, such as gold, which has a utility in itself for other purposes, aside from its use as money, the strict statement of the theory, though fundamentally unchanged, is a little complicated. In present circumstances we can excuse ourselves this complication. A currency note has no utility in itself and is completely worthless except for the purchasing power which it has as money.

Consequently what the public want is not so many ounces or so many square yards or even so many £ sterling of currency notes, but a quantity sufficient to cover a week's wages, or to pay their bills, or to meet their probable outgoings on a journey or a day's shopping. When people find themselves with more cash than they require for such purposes, they get rid of the surplus by buying goods or investments, or by leaving it for a bank to employ, or, possibly, by increasing their hoarded reserves. Thus the *number* of notes which the public ordinarily have on hand is determined by the amount of *purchasing power* which it suits them to hold or to carry about, and by nothing else. The amount of this purchasing power depends partly on their wealth, partly on their habits. The wealth of the public in the aggregate will only change gradually. Their habits in the use of money—whether their income is paid them weekly or monthly or quarterly, whether they pay cash at shops or run accounts, whether they deposit with banks, whether they cash small cheques at short intervals or larger cheques at longer intervals, whether they keep a reserve or hoard of money about the house— are more easily altered. But if their wealth and their habits in the above respects are unchanged, then the amount of purchasing power which they hold in the form of money is definitely fixed. We can measure this definite amount of purchasing power in terms of a unit made up of a collection of specified quantities of their standard articles of consumption or other objects of expenditure; for example, the kinds and quantities of articles which are combined for the purpose of a cost-of-living index number. Let us call such a unit a 'consumption unit' and assume that the public require to hold an amount of money having a purchasing power over k consumption units. Let there be n currency notes or other forms of cash in circulation with the public, and let p be the price of each consumption unit (i.e. p is the index number of the cost of living), then it follows from the above that $n = pk$. This is the famous quantity theory of money. So long as k remains unchanged, n and p rise and fall together; that is to say, the greater or the fewer the number of currency notes, the higher or the lower is the price level in the same proportion.

So far we have assumed that the whole of the public require-ment for purchasing power is satisfied by cash, and on the other hand that this requirement is the only source of demand for cash; neglecting the fact that the public, including the business world, employ for the same purpose bank deposits and over-draft facilities, whilst the banks must for the same reason main-tain a reserve of cash. The theory is easily extended, however, to cover this case. Let us assume that the public, including the business world, find it convenient to keep the equivalent of k consumption in cash and of a further k' available at their banks against cheques, and that the banks keep in cash a proportion r of their potential liabilities (k') to the public. Our equation then becomes
$$n = p(k + rk').$$

So long as k, k', and r remain unchanged, we have the same result as before, namely, that n and p rise and fall together. The proportion between k and k' depends on the banking arrange-ments of the public; the absolute value of these on their habits generally; and the value of r on the reserve practices of the banks. Thus, so long as these are unaltered, we still have a direct relation between the *quantity* of cash (n) and the level of prices (p).[1]

---

[1] My exposition follows the general lines of Professor Pigou (*Quarterly Journal of Economics*, November 1917) and of Dr Marshall (*Money, Credit, and Commerce*, I, iv), rather than the perhaps more familiar analysis of Professor Irving Fisher. Instead of starting with the amount of cash held by the public, Professor Fisher begins with the volume of business transacted by means of money and the frequency with which each unit of money changes hands. It comes to the same thing in the end and it is easy to pass from the above formula to Professor Fisher's; but the above method of approach seems less artificial than Professor Fisher's and nearer to the observed facts.

We have seen that the amount of k and k' depends partly on the wealth of the community, partly on its habits. Its habits are fixed by its estimation of the extra convenience of having more cash in hand as compared with the advantages to be got from spending the cash or investing it. The point of equilibrium is reached where the estimated advantages of keeping more cash in hand compared with those of spending or investing it about balance. The matter cannot be summed up better than in the words of Dr Marshall:

In every state of society there is some fraction of their income which people find it worth while to keep in the form of currency; it may be a fifth, or a tenth, or a twentieth. A large command of resources in the form of currency renders their business easy and smooth, and puts them at an advantage in bargaining; but on the other hand it locks up in a barren form resources that might yield an income of gratification if invested, say, in extra furniture; or a money income, if invested in extra machinery or cattle. A man fixes the appropriate fraction 'after balancing one against another the advantages of a further ready command, and the disadvantages of putting more of his resources into a form in which they yield him no direct income or other benefit'. 'Let us suppose that the inhabitants of a country, taken one with another (and including therefore all varieties of character and of occupation), find it just worth their while to keep by them on the average ready purchasing power to the extent of a tenth part of their annual income, together with a fiftieth part of their property; then the aggregate value of the currency of the country will tend to be equal to the sum of these amounts.'[1]

So far there should be no room for difference of opinion. The error often made by careless adherents of the quantity theory,

[1] *Money, Credit, and Commerce*, I, iv, 3. Dr Marshall shows in a footnote as follows that the above is in fact a development of the traditional way of considering the matter: 'Petty thought that the money "sufficient for" the nation is "so much as will pay half a year's rent for all the lands of England and a quarter's rent of the Houseing, for a week's expense of all the people, and about a quarter of the value of all the exported commodities." Locke estimated that "one-fiftieth of wages and one-fourth of the landowner's income and one-twentieth part of the broker's yearly returns in ready money will be enough to drive the trade of any country". Cantillon (A.D. 1755), after a long and subtle study, concludes that the value needed is a ninth of the total produce of the country; or, what he takes to be the same thing, a third of the rent of the land. Adam Smith has more of the scepticism of the modern age and says: "it is impossible to determine the proportion", though "it has been computed by different authors at a fifth, at a tenth, at a twentieth, and at a thirtieth part of the whole value of the annual produce."' In modern conditions the normal proportion of the circulation to this national income seems to be somewhere between a tenth and a fifteenth.

which may partly explain why it is not universally accepted, is as follows.

Every one admits that the habits of the public in the use of money and of banking facilities and the practices of the banks in respect of their reserves change from time to time as the result of obvious developments. These habits and practices are a reflection of changes in economic and social organisation. But the theory has often been expounded on the further assumption that a *mere* change in the quantity of the currency cannot affect k, r, and k'—that is to say, in mathematical parlance, that n is an *independent variable* in relation to these quantities. It would follow from this that an arbitrary doubling of n, since this in itself is assumed not to affect k, r, and k', must have the effect of raising p to double what it would have been otherwise. The quantity theory is often stated in this, or a similar, form.

Now 'in the long run' this is probably true. If, after the American Civil War, the American dollar had been stabilised and defined by law at 10 per cent below its present value, it would be safe to assume that n and p would now be just 10 per cent greater than they actually are and that the present values of k, r, and k' would be entirely unaffected. But this *long run* is a misleading guide to current affairs. *In the long run* we are all dead. Economists set themselves too easy, too useless a task if in tempestuous seasons they can only tell us that when the storm is long past the ocean is flat again.

In actual experience, a change of n is liable to have a reaction both on k and k' and on r. It will be enough to give a few typical instances. Before the war (and indeed since) there was a considerable element of what was conventional and arbitrary in the reserve policy of the banks, but especially in the policy of the state banks towards their gold reserves. These reserves were kept for show rather than for use, and their amount was not the result of close reasoning. There was a decided tendency on the part of these banks between 1900 and 1914 to bottle up gold when it flowed towards them and to part with it reluctantly when the tide was flowing the other way. Consequently, when gold became relatively abundant they tended to hoard what came their way and to raise the proportion of the reserves, with the result that the increased output of South African gold was absorbed with less effect on the price level than would have been the case if an increase of n had been totally without reaction on the value of r.

In agricultural countries where peasants readily hoard money, an inflation, especially in its early stages, does not raise prices proportionately, because when, as a result of a certain rise in the price of agricultural products, more money flows into the pockets of the peasants, it tends to stick there; deeming themselves that much richer, the peasants increase the proportion of their receipts that they hoard.

Thus in these and in other ways the terms of our equation tend in their movements to favour the stability of p, and there is a certain friction which prevents a moderate change in n from exercising its full proportionate effect on p.

On the other hand a large change in n, which rubs away the initial friction, and especially a change in n due to causes which set up a general expectation of a further change in the same direction, may produce a *more* than proportionate effect on p. After the general analysis of chapter 1 and the narratives of catastrophic inflations given in chapter 2, it is scarcely necessary to illustrate this further—it is a matter more readily understood than it was ten years ago. A large change in p greatly affects individual fortunes. Hence a change after it has occurred, or sooner in so far as it is anticipated, may greatly affect the monetary habits of the public in their attempt to protect themselves from a similar loss in future, or to make gains and avoid loss during the passage from the equilibrium corresponding to the old value of n to the equilibrium corresponding to its new value. Thus after, during, and (so far as the change is anticipated) before a change in the value of n, there will be some reaction on the values of k, k', and r, with the result that the change in the value of p, at least temporarily and perhaps permanently (since habits and practices, once changed, will not revert to exactly their old shape), will not be precisely in proportion to the change in n.

The terms *inflation* and *deflation* are used by different writers in varying senses. It would be convenient to speak of an increase or decrease in n as an inflation or deflation of *cash*; and of a decrease or increase in r as an inflation or deflation of *credit*. The characteristic of the 'credit cycle' (as the alternation of boom and depression is now described) consists in a tendency of k and k' to diminish during the boom and increase during the depression, irrespective of changes in n and r, these movements representing respectively a diminution and an increase of 'real' balances (i.e. balances, in hand or at the bank, measured in terms of purchasing power); so that we might call this phenomenon deflation and inflation of real balances.

It will illustrate the 'quantity theory' equation in general and the phenomena of deflation and inflation of real balances in particular, if we endeavour to fill in actual values for our symbolic quantities. The following example does not claim to be exact and its object is to illustrate the idea rather than to convey statistically precise facts. October 1920 was about the end of the recent boom, and October 1922 was near the bottom of the depression. At these two dates the figures of price level (taking October 1922 as 100), cash circulation (note circulation *plus* private deposits at the Bank of England),[1] and bank deposits in Great Britain were roughly as follows:

	Price level	Cash circulation (£ million)	Bank deposits (£ million)
October 1920	150	585	2,000
October 1922	100	504	1,700

The value of r was not very different at the two dates—say about 12 per cent. Consequently our equation for the two dates works out as follows:[2]

$$\text{October 1920} \quad n = 585 \quad p = 1\cdot5 \quad k = 230 \quad k' = 1{,}333$$
$$\text{October 1922} \quad n = 504 \quad p = 1 \quad k = 300 \quad k' = 1{,}700$$

---

[1] It would take me too far from the immediate matter in hand to discuss why I take this definition of 'cash' in the case of Great Britain. It is discussed further in chapter 5 below.

[2] For $585 = 1\cdot5(230 + 1{,}333 \times 0\cdot12)$, and $504 = 1(300 + 1{,}700 \times 0\cdot12)$.

Thus during the depression k rose from 230 to 300 and k' from 1,333 to 1,700, which means that the cash holdings of the public at the former date were worth $\frac{22}{30}$, and their bank balances $\frac{1333}{1700}$, of what they were worth at the latter date. It thus appears that the tendency of k and k' to increase had more to do than the deflation of 'cash' had with the fall of prices between the two periods. If k and k' were to fall back to their 1920 values, prices would rise 30 per cent without any change whatever in the volume of cash or the reserve policy of the banks. Thus even in Great Britain the fluctuations of k and k' can have a decisive influence on the price level; whilst we have already seen (pp. 45, 46) how enormously they can change in the recent conditions of Russia and Central Europe.

The moral of this discussion, to be carried forward in the reader's mind until we reach chapters 4 and 5, is that the price level is not mysterious, but is governed by a few, definite, analysable influences. Two of these, n and r, are under the direct control (or ought to be) of the central banking authorities. The third, namely k and k', is not directly controllable, and depends on the mood of the public and the business world. The business of stabilising the price level, not merely over long periods but so as also to avoid cyclical fluctuations, consists partly in exercising a stabilising influence over k and k', and, in so far as this fails or is impracticable, in deliberately varying n and r so as to *counterbalance* the movement of k and k'.

The usual method of exercising a stabilising influence over k and k', especially over k', is that of bank rate. A tendency of k' to increase may be somewhat counteracted by lowering the bank rate, because easy lending diminishes the advantage of keeping a margin for contingencies in cash. Cheap money also operates to *counterbalance* an increase of k', because, by encouraging borrowing from the banks, it prevents r from increasing or causes r to diminish. But it is doubtful whether bank rate by itself is always a powerful enough instrument, and, if we are to achieve stability, we must be prepared to vary n and r on occasion.

Our analysis suggests that the first duty of the central banking and currency authorities is to make sure that they have n and r thoroughly under control. For example, so long as inflationary taxation is in question n will be influenced by other than currency objects and cannot, therefore, be fully under control; moreover, at the other extreme, under a gold standard n is not always under control, because it depends on the unregulated forces which determine the demand and supply of gold throughout the world. Again, without a central banking system r will not be under proper control because it will be determined by the unco-ordinated decisions of numerous different banks.

At the present time in Great Britain r is very completely controlled, and n also, so long as we refrain from inflationary finance on the one hand and from a return to an unregulated gold standard on the other.[1] The second duty of the authorities is therefore worth discussing, namely, the *use* of their control over n and r to counterbalance changes in k and k'. Even if k and k' were entirely outside the influence of deliberate policy, which is not in fact the case, nevertheless p could be kept reasonably steady by suitable modifications of the values of n and r.

Old-fashioned advocates of sound money have laid too much emphasis on the need of keeping n and r steady, and have argued as if this policy by itself would produce the right results. So far from this being so, steadiness of n and r, when k and k' are not steady, is bound to lead to unsteadiness of the price level. Cyclical fluctuations are characterised, not primarily by changes in n or r, but by changes in k and k'. It follows that they can only be cured if we are ready deliberately to increase and decrease n and r, when symptoms of movement are showing in the values of k and k'. I am being led, however, into a large subject beyond my immediate purpose, and am anticipating also the topic of chapter 5. These hints will serve, nevertheless, to indicate to the

[1] In the case of the United States the same thing is more or less true, so long as the Federal Reserve Board is prepared to incur the expense of bottling up redundant gold.

reader what a long way we may be led by an understanding of the implications of the simple quantity equation with which we started.

2. *The theory of purchasing power parity*

The quantity theory deals with the purchasing power or commodity value of a given national currency. We come now to the *relative* value of *two* distinct national currencies, that is to say, to the theory of the foreign exchanges.

When[1] the currencies of the world[2] were nearly all on a gold basis, their relative value (i.e. the exchanges) depended on the actual amount of gold metal in a unit of each, with minor adjustments for the cost of transferring the metal from place to place.

When this common measure has ceased to be effective and we have instead a number of independent systems of inconvertible paper, what basic fact determines the rates at which units of the different currencies exchange for one another?[3]

[1] At this point the text begins to follow his article of 20 April 1922, 'The Theory of the Exchanges and "Purchasing Power Parity"'.

[2] The words 'the world' in the text replaced the word 'Europe' in the article.

[3] At this point the texts diverge until the words 'we find' on page 71. The article runs as follows: 'It is dull and useless to say that "it depends on supply and demand". Can we not carry the analysis a little further and enable the ordinary imagination to visualise the process?

'The explanation most popular at present amongst writers on this subject, and, properly understood, perhaps the most correct, is the doctrine with which Professor Cassel has familiarised the public under the name of "Purchasing power parity".

'Without wishing to criticise overmuch the more careful exponents of this doctrine (for whose views the reader may be referred to the articles by Professor Cassel, Professor Pigou, and Mr Bickerdike which have appeared from time to time in the *Economic Journal*), I fancy that by becoming a patter-phrase it is getting responsible for confusing more minds than it enlightens. Many, using it as a mere counter, a substitute, not an instrument, of thought, are not a penny the wiser for repeating it, and possibly, if they are interested in the exchanges, a mark the poorer!

'We must begin by introducing the distinction between a currency's "internal" and "external" purchasing power. Consider the price in marks in Germany of a block of standard commodities—that price may be taken to measure the "internal" purchasing power of the mark; if, after an interval of time, that price rises, then the internal purchasing power of the mark has proportionately fallen. Consider next the price in marks which would have to be paid if, instead of that block of commodities being bought in Germany, a similar block of commodities was purchased abroad with foreign currency, this foreign currency being obtained by selling marks over the exchanges—that price measures the "external" purchasing power of the mark.

'Now the basis of the doctrine of purchasing power parity (paraphrasing Professor Pigou's statement of it) is that, in ordinary conditions of trade equilibrium, Germans

The explanation is to be found in the doctrine, as old in itself as Ricardo, with which Professor Cassel has lately familiarised the public under the name of 'purchasing power parity'.[1]

This doctrine in its baldest form runs as follows. (1) The purchasing power of an inconvertible currency within its own country, i.e. the currency's *internal* purchasing power, depends on the currency policy of the government and the currency habits of the people, in accordance with the quantity theory of money just discussed. (2) The purchasing power of an inconvertible currency in a foreign country, i.e. the currency's *external* purchasing power, must be the rate of exchange between the home currency and the foreign currency, multiplied by the foreign currency's purchasing power in its own country. (3) In conditions of equilibrium the *internal* and *external* purchasing powers of a currency must be the *same*, allowance being made for transport charges and import and export taxes; for otherwise a movement of trade would occur in order to take advantage of the inequality. (4) It follows, therefore, from (1), (2), and (3) that the rate of exchange between the home currency and the foreign currency must tend in equilibrium to be the ratio between the purchasing powers of the home currency at home and of the foreign currency in the foreign country. This ratio between the respective home purchasing powers of the two currencies is designated their 'purchasing power parity'.

If, therefore, we find that the internal and external purchasing powers of the home currency are widely different, and, which is

cannot be paying different quantities of marks per unit for the same commodities as sold in Germany and as sold, *allowance being made for transport charges and import or export taxes*, in America. From this it follows that, if there were no transport charges, &c., the external and internal purchasing power of marks *in respect of goods entering into international trade* must always, in equilibrium, be equal. The ratio given by the price in marks of the block of standard commodities in Germany divided by the price in dollars of the same commodities in America yields an exchange value for marks in terms of dollars which we may call the "purchasing power parity". In equilibrium, so the doctrine runs, the purchasing power parity thus calculated must tend to be equal to the exchange rate between marks and dollars actually quoted by the dealers. If, on the other hand,'

[1] [This term was first introduced into economic literature in an article contributed by Professor Cassel to the *Economic Journal*, December 1918. For Professor Cassel's considered opinions on the whole question, see his *Money and Foreign Exchange after 1914* (1922). The theory, as distinct from the name, is essentially Ricardo's.]

71

the same thing, that the actual exchange rates differ widely from the purchasing power parities,[1] then we are justified in inferring that equilibrium is not established, and that, as time goes on, forces will come into play to bring the actual exchange rates and the purchasing power parities nearer together. The actual exchanges are often more sensitive and more volatile than the purchasing power parities, being subject to speculation, to sudden movements of funds, to seasonal influences,[2] and to *anticipations* of impending changes in purchasing power parity (due to relative inflation or deflation); though also on other occasions they may lag behind. Nevertheless it is the purchasing power parity, according to this doctrine, which[3] corresponds to the old gold par. This[4] is the point about which the exchanges fluctuate, and[5] at which they must ultimately come to rest;[6] with

[1] In the original article the word 'parity' replaces 'parities' in this and the next sentence.
[2] The words 'to seasonal influences' do not appear in the article.
[3] In the article, the early part of this sentence reads: 'But the purchasing power parity'.
[4] In the article, a semi-colon follows 'par' and 'it' replaces 'This'.
[5] In the article 'but' replaces 'and'.
[6] At this point the texts diverge markedly, coming together at the second sentence of the second paragraph on page 74. The article continues as follows:

'The doctrine as generally expounded does not entirely overlook the fact that owing to costs of transport, tariffs, and other causes internal and external purchasing power never were, even in times of equilibrium, exactly equal. But this difficulty is overcome by taking some base period, generally the year 1913, and assuming that the percentage difference between internal and external purchasing power at that date may be taken as an approximately satisfactory correction for the same disturbing factors at the present time. For example, instead of calculating directly the cost of a standard set of goods at home and abroad respectively, the calculations are made that $16\frac{1}{2}$ marks are required to buy in Germany a standard set which one mark would have bought in 1914, and that £2 are required to buy in England what £1 would have bought in 1914. On this basis (the pre-war purchasing power parity being assumed to be correctly measured by 20 marks = £1) the present purchasing power parity of marks and sterling is $20 \times 16\frac{1}{2} \div 2 = 165$. If the actual rate of exchange is 1,000, this shows an enormous divergence from purchasing power parity, the internal value of the mark being no less than six times its external value.

'At first sight this theory appears to be one of great practical utility; and some of those numerous persons who are interested in trying to forecast the exchanges have, during the last two years, prepared charts for themselves exhibiting the divergences between the actual exchange rates and the purchasing power parities, and have been disposed to draw from such charts important practical conclusions.

'Such charts are of high interest, as I confess by printing a good collection of them at the conclusion of this article. But it is necessary to add that the drawing of inferences from such charts is difficult and obscure, and that the popular use of them is full of error.

'Let the reader cast his eyes back to the words italicised above, to the effect that the theory, in the form in which it has been stated above, must only be applied in respect of goods entering into international trade, and must allow for transport and tariff costs.

72

one material difference, namely, that it is not itself a fixed point—since, if internal prices move differently in the two countries under comparison, the purchasing power parity also moves, so that equilibrium may be restored, not only by a movement in the market rate of exchange, but also by a movement of the purchasing power parity itself.

At first sight this theory appears to be one of great practical utility; and many persons have endeavoured to draw important practical conclusions about the future course of the exchanges from charts exhibiting the divergences between the market rate of exchange and the purchasing power parities—undeterred by the perplexity whether an existing divergence from equilibrium will be remedied by a movement of the exchanges or of the purchasing power parity or of both.

In practical applications of the doctrine there are, however, two further difficulties, which we have allowed so far to escape our attention, both of them arising out of the words *allowance being made for transport charges and import and export taxes*. The first difficulty is how to make allowance for such charges and taxes. The second difficulty is how to treat purchasing power over goods and services which *do not enter into international trade at all*.

The doctrine, in the form in which it is generally applied, endeavours to deal with the first difficulty by assuming that the percentage difference between internal and external purchasing power at some standard date, when approximate equilibrium may be presumed to have existed, generally the year 1913, may

Practical applications of the theory are nearly always along different lines from this; for the standard set of commodities selected is not confined to goods which are exported from and imported into the countries under comparison, but is generally the same set as is used for the purpose of index numbers of general purchasing power or of the working-class cost of living. Moreover, tariff costs, if this term is taken to cover all export and import regulations, including prohibitions and official or semi-official combines for differentiating between export and home prices, are notoriously widely different in many cases from those which existed in 1913.

'Thus a part of the divergence between purchasing power parities, as commonly calculated, and actual exchange rates may be explained by the fact that the calculations are not strictly in accordance with the theory as precisely enunciated.'

be taken as an approximately satisfactory correction for the same disturbing factors at the present time. For example, instead of calculating directly the cost of a standard set of goods at home and abroad respectively, the calculations are made that $2 are required to buy in the United States a standard set which $1 would have bought in 1913, and that £2.43 are required to buy in England what £1 would have bought in 1913. On this basis (the pre-war purchasing power parity being assumed to be in equilibrium with the pre-war exchange of $4.86 = £1) the present purchasing power parity between dollars and sterling is given by $4 = £1, since $4.86 \times 2 \div 2.43 = 4$.

The obvious objection to this method of correction is that transport and tariff costs, especially if this term is taken to cover all export and import regulations, including prohibitions and official or semi-official combines for differentiating between export and home prices, are notoriously widely different in many cases from those which existed in 1913. We should not get the same result if we were to take some year other than 1913 as the basis of the calculation.

The second difficulty—the treatment of purchasing power over articles which do not enter into international trade—is still more serious. For,[1] if we restrict[2] ourselves to articles entering into international trade and make[3] exact allowance for transport and tariff costs, we should find that the theory is always in accordance with[4] the facts, with perhaps a short time-lag,[5] the purchasing power parity being[6] never very far from the market rate of exchange.[7] Indeed,[8] it is the whole business of the international merchant to see that this is so; for[9] whenever the rates are temporarily out of parity he is in a position to make a profit

---

[1] The word 'for' in the text replaces the word 'indeed' in the article.
[2] In the article 'restrict' is past tense.   [3] In the article 'make' is past tense.
[4] The words 'always in accordance with' in the text replace the words 'borne out by' in the article.
[5] In the article 'and' appears here.
[6] The word 'being' in the text replaces the word 'is' in the article.
[7] The words 'market rate of exchange' in the text replace the words 'actual exchange rate' in the article.   [8] The word 'indeed' is unique to the text.
[9] The word 'for' in the text replaces the word 'and' in the article.

by moving goods. The prices of cotton in New York, Liverpool, Havre, Hamburg, Genoa, and Prague, expressed in dollars, sterling, francs, marks, lire, and krone respectively, are never for any length of time much divergent from one another on the basis of the exchange rates actually obtaining in the market, due allowance being made for tariffs and the cost of moving cotton from one centre to another; and the same is true of other articles of international trade, though with an increasing time-lag as we pass to articles which are not standardised or are not handled in organised markets. In fact, the theory, stated thus, is a truism, and as nearly as possible jejune.[1]

For this reason practical applications of the theory are not thus restricted. The standard set of commodities selected is not confined to goods which are exported from and imported into the countries under comparison, but is the same set, generally speaking, as is used for compiling index numbers of general purchasing power or of the working-class cost of living. Yet applied in this way[2]—namely, in a comparison of movements of the *general*[3] index numbers of home prices in two countries with movements in the rates of exchange between their currencies— the theory[4] requires a further assumption for its validity, namely, that in the long run the home prices of the goods and services which do not enter into international trade, move in more or less the same proportions as those which do.[5]

So far from this being a truism, it is not literally or exactly true at all; and one can only say that it is more or less true according to circumstances. If capital and labour can freely move on

---

[1] In the article, this sentence, which started the next paragraph, runs 'In fact, the theory of purchasing power parity, as stated above, is a truism (just like the quantity theory of money), and as nearly as possible jejune.'

[2] This paragraph up to here replaces the words 'Hence the theory, as it is usually applied' in the article.

[3] The word 'general' is not italicised in the article.

[4] The words 'the theory' do not appear at this point in the article.

[5] ['Our calculation of the purchasing power parity rests strictly on the proviso that the rise in prices in the countries concerned has affected all commodities in a like degree. If that proviso is not fulfilled, then the actual exchange rate may deviate from the calculated purchasing power parity.' Cassel, *Money and Foreign Exchange after 1914*, p. 154.]

a large scale between home and export industries without loss of relative efficiency, if[1] there is no movement in the 'equation of exchange' (see below) with the other country, and if the fluctuations in price are solely due to monetary influences and not to changes in other economic relationships between the two countries, then this[2] further assumption may be approximately justified. But this is not always the case; and such a cataclysm as the war, with its various consequences to victor and vanquished, may set up a new equilibrium position. There may, for example, be a change more or less permanent, or at least as prolonged as the reparation payments, in the relative exchange values[3] of Germany's imports and exports respectively, or of those German products and services which can enter into international trade and those which cannot. Or,[4] again, the strengthening of the financial position of the United States as against Europe, which has resulted from the war, may have shifted the old equilibrium in a direction favourable to the United States. In such cases[5] it is not correct to assume that the coefficients of purchasing power parity, calculated, as they generally are calculated,[6] by means of the relative variations of index numbers of general purchasing power from their pre-war levels, must ultimately approximate to the actual rates of exchange, or that internal and external purchasing power must ultimately bear to one another the same relation as in 1913.

The[7] index number calculated for the United States by the Federal Reserve Board illustrates how disturbing may be the

[1] The words from 'if' to 'countries' in the text replace the words 'and if the real wages of labour in the two countries under comparison are not changing relatively to one another, the fluctuations in price being due to monetary influences and not to changes in other economic conditions' in the article.

[2] The word 'this' in the text replaces the word 'the' in the article.

[3] In the article, the rest of this sentence runs 'between German products and services and those of other countries'.

[4] This sentence does not appear in the article.

[5] The words 'such cases' in the text replace the words 'this case' in the article.

[6] The words 'by means of the relative variations of index numbers of general purchasing power from their pre-war levels' in the text replace the words 'in the tables given below' in the article.

[7] This paragraph does not appear in the article.

influence of the change since 1913 in the relative prices of imported goods, exported goods, and commodities generally:

	Goods imported	Goods exported	All commodities
1913	100	100	100
July 1922	128	165	165
April 1923	156	186	169
July 1923	141	170	159

Thus the theory does not provide a simple or ready-made measure of the 'true' value of the exchanges. When it is restricted to foreign-trade goods,[1] it is little better than a truism. When[2] it is not so restricted, the conception of purchasing power parity becomes much more interesting, but is no longer an accurate forecaster of the course of the foreign exchanges. If, therefore, we follow the ordinary practice of fixing purchasing power parity by comparisons of the *general* purchasing power of a country's currency at home and abroad, then we must not infer from this

---

[1] The words 'when it is restricted to foreign-trade goods' in the text replace the words 'if it is interpreted one way' in the article.

[2] At this point, the text and the article diverge and do not come together until the third sentence of the first paragraph on page 78. In the interim, the article runs as follows:

'If it is interpreted the other way, it becomes decidedly interesting, but no longer exact in relation to the exchanges.

'Since we must decide which way we are going to interpret it, I prefer the more interesting definition—that is to say, the definition which does not limit the relevance of purchasing power parity to the articles which enter into international trade (in respect of which its equivalence with the actual exchange rates is a truism), but employs it to measure variations in the general purchasing power of a country's currency at home and abroad. This definition, precisely stated for the case of Germany and England, is as follows:

'At the base period (generally 1913) let us assume that there was an exchange of £1 = 20 marks, and that our index numbers of the general purchasing power of £1 in England and of one mark in Germany stood respectively at 100. If at the present time (1922) the English index number has increased to 200 and the German index number to 1,650, then the purchasing power parity between sterling and marks, with 1913 as our base, is $20 \times 1,650 \div 200 = 165$.

'But we must not infer from this that the exchange between sterling and marks ought to stand at £1 = 165 marks, or that it is only a matter of time before the purchasing power parity and the actual rate of exchange return to an approximate equality. It will be observed that our definition essentially introduces a base year. If we had chosen a different base year (e.g. 1919) we should have got a different answer. Purchasing power parity, thus defined, tells us an important fact about the relative changes in the purchasing power of money in England and Germany between 1913 and 1922, but it does not lay down a law as to what the equilibrium exchange rate between sterling and marks in 1922 ought to be.

'Thus defined "purchasing power parity" becomes decidedly interesting, partly for its bearing on the exchanges, partly for other reasons. The critical scepticism expressed above about its relation to the actual rate of exchange must not be carried too far.'

that the actual rate of exchange *ought* to stand at the purchasing power parity, or that it is only a matter of time and adjustment before the two will return to equality. Purchasing power parity, thus defined, tells us an important fact about the relative changes in the purchasing power of money in (e.g.) England and the United States or Germany between 1913 and, say, 1923, but it does not necessarily settle what the equilibrium exchange rate in 1923 between sterling and dollars or marks ought to be.

Thus defined 'purchasing power parity' deserves attention, even though it is not always an accurate forecaster of the foreign exchanges. The practical importance of our qualifications must not be exaggerated. If the fluctuations of purchasing power parity are markedly different from the fluctuations in the exchanges, this indicates an actual or impending change in the relative prices of the two classes of goods which respectively do and do not enter into international trade. Now there is certainly a tendency for movements in the prices of these two classes of goods to influence one another in the long run. The relative valuation placed on them is derived from deep economic and psychological causes which are not easily disturbed. If, therefore,[1] the divergence from the pre-existing equilibrium is mainly[2] due to monetary causes (as, for example, different degrees of inflation or deflation in the two countries), as it often is,[3] then we may reasonably[4] expect that purchasing power parity and exchange value will come together again before long.[5]

When this is the case,[6] it is not possible to say in general[7] whether exchange value will move towards purchasing power parity or the other way round. Sometimes, as recently in Europe,[8]

[1] The word 'therefore' does not appear in the article.
[2] The word 'mainly' in the text replaces the word 'entirely' in the article.
[3] The words 'as it often is' in the text do not appear in the article.
[4] The word 'reasonably' does not appear in the article.
[5] The words 'before long' in the text replace the words 'sooner or later' in the article.
[6] The words 'When this is the case' do not appear in the article.
[7] The words 'in general' in the text replace the words 'without reference to each particular case' in the article.
[8] The words 'as recently in Europe' in the text replace the words 'and especially in the recent circumstances of Europe' in the article.

it is the exchanges which are the more sensitive to impending relative price changes[1] and move first; whilst in other cases[2] the exchanges may not move until after the change in the relation between the internal and external price levels is an accomplished fact. But[3] the essence of the purchasing power parity theory, considered as an explanation of the exchanges, is to be found, I think,[4] in its regarding internal purchasing power as being in the long run a more trustworthy indicator[5] of a currency's[6] value[7] than the market rates of exchange, because internal purchasing power quickly reflects the monetary policy of the country, which is the final determinant. If the market rates of exchange fall[8] further than the country's existing or impending currency policy justifies by[9] its effect on the internal purchasing power of the country's money, then sooner or later the exchange value is bound to recover. Thus, provided no persisting change is taking place in the basic economic relations between two countries, and provided the internal purchasing power of the currency has in each country settled down to equilibrium in relation to the currency policy of the authorities, then[10] the rate of exchange between the currencies of the two countries must also settle down[11] in the long run to correspond with[12] their comparative internal purchasing powers. Subject to these assumptions[13] comparative internal purchasing power does take the place of the old gold

---

[1] The words 'relative price changes' in the text replace the word 'events' in the article.

[2] In the article, the words 'the opposite is true' replaces the rest of this sentence.

[3] In the article, the words 'it may be said, I think, that' are added here.

[4] The words 'I think' in the text do not appear here in the article.

[5] The words 'a more trustworthy indicator' in the text replace the words 'the more fundamental determinant' in the article.

[6] In the article, the words 'foreign exchange' follow the word 'currency's'.

[7] The rest of this sentence in the article runs 'internal purchasing power in its turn being fixed by the monetary policy of the authorities, whether inflationist or deflationist, this being the ultimate determiner'.

[8] The words 'If the market rates of exchange fall' in the text replace the words 'If the exchange value falls' in the article.

[9] The word 'by' in the text replaces the word 'in' in the article.

[10] In the article, the words 'a modification in' follow the word 'then'.

[11] The words 'also settle down' in the text replace the word 'correspond' in the article.

[12] The words 'correspond with' in the text replace the words 'modifications in' in the article.

[13] The word 'assumptions' in the text replaces the word 'provisoes' in the article.

parity as furnishing the point about which the short-period[1] movements of the exchanges fluctuate.

If, on the other hand,[2] these assumptions[3] are not fulfilled and changes are taking place in the 'equation of exchange',[4] as economists call it, between the services and products of one country and those of another, either on account of movements of capital, or reparation payments, or changes in the relative efficiency of labour, or changes in the urgency of the world's demand for that country's special products,[5] or the like, then the equilibrium point between purchasing power parity and the rate of exchange may be modified[6] permanently.

This[7] point may be made clearer by an example. Let us consider two countries, Westropa and the United States of the Hesperides, and let us assume for the sake of simplicity, and also because it may often correspond to the facts, that in both countries the price of exported goods moves in the same way as the price of other home-produced goods, but that the 'equation of exchange' has moved in favour of the Hesperides so that a smaller number than before of units of Hesperidean products exchange for a given quantity of Westropean products. It follows from this that imported products in Westropa will rise in price more than commodities generally, whilst in the Hesperides they will rise less. Let us suppose that between 1913 and 1923 the Westropean index number of prices has risen from 100 to 155 and the Hesperidean index number from 100 to 160; that these index numbers are so constructed in each case that imported commodities constitute 20 per cent and home-produced commodities 80 per cent of the whole; and that the 'equation of exchange'

[1] The rest of this sentence in the article runs 'fluctuations of the exchanges must swing'.
[2] The words 'on the other hand' in the text replace the word 'however' in the article.
[3] The word 'assumptions' in the text replaces the word 'provisoes' in the article.
[4] The phrase 'equation of exchange' is not in quotation marks in the article.
[5] The following additional examples appear in the article: 'or a breakdown of pre-existing organisation, or a fall in the standard of life'.
[6] The words 'more or less' follow the word 'modified' in the article.
[7] At this point the article and the text diverge in presentation although not greatly in content. The rest of the article, which discusses changes in purchasing power parity up to December 1921 for England, France, Italy, Germany and Sweden, appears as Appendix II.

has moved 10 per cent in favour of the Hesperides, that is to say a given quantity of the goods exported by the Hesperides will buy 10 per cent more than before of the goods exported by Westropa. The state of affairs is then as follows:[1]

Westropa: Price index of
imported commodities (x) 167
home-produced commodities (y) 152
all commodities   155

Hesperides: Price index of
imported commodities (x') 148
home-produced commodities (y') 163
all commodities   160

Thus it appears that the purchasing power parity of the Westropean currency in 1923 compared with 1913 is $\left(\frac{160}{155}=\right)$ 103; whereas the rate of exchange, compared with the 1913 parity, is $\left(\frac{163}{167}=\frac{148}{152}=\right)$ 97. If the worsening of Westropa's equation of exchange with the Hesperides is permanent, then its purchasing power parity (on the 1913 basis) will also remain permanently above the equilibrium value of the market rate of exchange.

A tendency of these two measures of the value of a country's currency to move differently is, therefore, a highly interesting symptom. If the market rate of exchange shows a continuing tendency to stand below the purchasing power parity, we have, failing any other explanation, some reason to suspect a worsening of the 'equation of exchange' as compared with the base year.

In the charts and tables below, the actual results are worked out of applying the theory to the exchange value of sterling, francs, and lire in terms of dollars since 1919. The figures show that, quantitatively speaking, the influences which detract from the precision of the purchasing power parity theory have been in these cases small, on the whole, as compared with those which function in accord with it. There seems to have been some disturbance in the 'equations of exchange' since 1913—which would probably show up more distinctly if it were not that the index numbers employed in the following enquiry are of the

[1]   [For $10x = 11y$ $11x' = 10y'$
          $8y + 2x = 1550$ $8y' + 2x' = 1600.$]

type which is largely built up from articles entering into international trade. Nevertheless general price changes, affecting all commodities more or less equally, due to currency inflation or deflation, have been so dominant in their influence that the theory has been actually applicable with remarkable accuracy. In the case, however, of such countries as Germany, where the shocks to equilibrium have been much more violent in many respects, the concordance between the purchasing power parity based on 1913 and the actual rate of exchange has suffered, whether temporarily or permanently, very great disturbance.

The first of these charts, which deals with the value of sterling in terms of dollars, shows that whilst the purchasing power parity, calculated with 1913 as base, is often somewhat above the actual exchange, there is a persevering tendency for the two to come together. The two curves are within one point of each other in September–November 1919, March–April 1920, April 1921, September 1921, January–June 1922, and February–June 1923, which is certainly a remarkable illustration of the tendency to concordance between the purchasing power parity and the rate of exchange. On inductive grounds it would be tempting to conclude from this chart that the financial consequences of the war have depressed the equilibrium of the purchasing power parity of sterling as against the dollar from 1 to $2\frac{1}{2}$ per cent since 1913, if it were not that this figure barely exceeds the margin of error resulting from the choice of one pair of index numbers rather than another from amongst those available.[1] It will be interesting to see what effect is produced by the payment, just commenced, of the interest on the American debt.

This chart brings out clearly, as also do those for France and Italy, the susceptibility of the foreign exchange rates to seasonal influences, whereas the purchasing power parity is naturally less affected by them.

In the case of France the curves are together at the end of

[1] [Nevertheless, if I had used the Board of Trade or the *Statist* index number in place of the *Economist* index number in the table below, the presumption of a slight worsening of the 'equation of exchange' against Great Britain would be somewhat strengthened.]

1919, diverge in 1920, come together again in the middle of 1921, and keep together until a divergence occurred again in the latter part of 1922.

For Italy, rather unexpectedly perhaps, the relationship is extraordinarily steady, although here, as in the case of France and Great Britain, there are indications that the war may have resulted in a slight lowering of the equilibrium point, by (say) 10 per cent;[1] the parity, calculated with 1913 as the base year, has been almost invariably somewhat above the actual rate of exchange. The Italian curve illustrates in a remarkable way the manner in which the external and internal purchasing powers of the currency fall together, when the main influence at work is a progressive depreciation due to currency inflation.

The broad effect of these curves and tables is to give substantial inductive support to the general theory outlined above, even under such abnormal conditions as have existed since the Armis-

[1] [The use of any of the other Italian index numbers would have accentuated this indication. The table of American prices given on p. 77 above confirms the suggestion that the 'equation of exchange' between the U.S. and the rest of the world as a whole has moved, say, 10 per cent in favour of the former.]

GREAT BRITAIN AND THE UNITED STATES

Per cent of 1913 parity	Price index number		Purchasing power parity[3]	Actual exchange (monthly average)
	Great Britain[1]	United States[2]		
1919				
August	242	216	89·3	87·6
September	245	210	85·7	85·8
October	252	211	83·7	85·9
November	259	217	83·8	84·3
December	273	223	81·7	78·4
1920				
January	289	233	81·0	75·6
February	303	232	76·7	69·5
March	310	234	75·6	76·2
April	306	245	80·1	80·6
May	305	247	81·0	79·0
June	291	243	83·5	81·1
July	293	241	82·3	79·4
August	288	231	80·2	74·2
September	284	226	79·6	72·2
October	266	211	79·3	71·4
November	246	196	79·7	70·7
December	220	179	81·4	71·4
1921				
January	209	170	81·4	76·7
February	192	160	83·3	79·6
March	189	155	82·0	80·3
April	183	148	80·9	80·7
May	182	145	79·7	81·5
June	179	142	79·3	78·0
July	178	141	79·2	74·8
August	179	142	79·3	75·1
September	183	141	77·0	76·5
October	170	142	83·5	79·5
November	166	141	84·9	81·5
December	162	140	86·4	85·3
1922				
January	159	138	86·8	86·8
February	158	141	89·1	89·6
March	160	142	88·7	89·9
April	159	143	89·9	90·7
May	162	148	91·4	91·4
June	163	150	92·0	91·5
July	163	155	95·1	91·4
August	158	155	98·1	91·7
September	156	153	98·1	91·1
October	158	154	97·4	91·2
November	159	156	98·1	92·0
December	158	156	98·7	94·6

GREAT BRITAIN AND THE UNITED STATES *(cont.)*

Per cent of 1913 parity	Price index number		Purchasing power parity[3]	Actual exchange (monthly average)
	Great Britain[1]	United States[2]		
1923				
January	160	156	97·5	95·7
February	163	157	96·3	96·2
March	163	159	97·5	96·5
April	165	159	96·4	95·7
May	164	156	95·1	95·0
June	160	153	95·6	94·8

[1] *Economist* index number.   [2] U.S. Bureau of Labour index number, as revised.
[3] The U.S. Bureau of Labour index number divided by the *Economist* index number.

FRANCE AND THE UNITED STATES

Per cent of 1913 parity	Purchasing power parity[1]	Actual exchange	Per cent of 1913 parity	Purchasing power parity[1]	Actual exchange
1919			**1921**		
August	62	66	August	43	40
September	58	61	September	41	38
October	55	60	October	43	38
November	53	55	November	42	37
December	52	48	December	43	40
1920			**1922**		
January	48	44	January	44	42
February	44	36	February	46	45
March	42	37	March	46	47
April	41	32	April	46	48
May	45	35	May	44	47
June	49	41	June	46	45
July	48	42	July	48	43
August	46	37	August	47	41
September	43	35	September	46	40
October	42	34	October	46	38
November	43	31	November	44	35
December	41	30	December	43	37
1921			**1923**		
January	42	33	January	40	34
February	42	37	February	37	32
March	43	36	March	37	33
April	43	37	April	38	35
May	44	43	May	38	34
June	44	42	June	37	33
July	43	40			

[1] U.S. Bureau of Labour index divided by French official wholesale index.

ITALY AND THE UNITED STATES

Per cent of 1913 parity	Purchasing power parity[1]	Actual exchange	Per cent of 1913 parity	Purchasing power parity[1]	Actual exchange
1919			**1921**		
August	59	56	August	26	22
September	56	53	September	24	22
October	54	51	October	24	20
November	50	44	November	24	21
December	49	40	December	23	23
1920			**1922**		
January	46	37	January	24	23
February	42	29	February	25	25
March	38	28	March	27	26
April	36	23	April	27	28
May	38	27	May	28	27
June	40	31	June	28	26
July	39	30	July	28	24
August	37	25	August	27	23
September	34	23	September	26	22
October	32	20	October	26	22
November	30	19	November	26	23
December	28	18	December	27	26
1921			**1923**		
January	26	18	January	27	26
February	26	19	February	27	25
March	26	20	March	27	25
April	25	24	April	27	26
May	27	27	May	27	25
June	28	26	June	26	24
July	27	24			

[1] U.S. Bureau of Labour index number divided by the 'Bachi' index number.

tice. During this period the movements of the relative price level in France and Italy due to monetary inflation have been so much larger than any shifting in the 'equation of exchange' (a movement of more than 10 or 20 per cent in which would be startling) that their foreign exchanges have been much more influenced by their internal price policy in relation to the internal price policies of other countries than by any other factor; with the result that the purchasing power parity theory, even in its crude form, has worked passably well.

3. *The seasonal fluctuation*

Thus the theory of purchasing power parity tells us that movements in the rate of exchange between the currencies of two countries tend, subject to adjustment in respect of movements in the 'equation of exchange', to correspond pretty closely to movements in the internal price levels of the two countries each expressed in their own currency. It follows that the rate of exchange can be improved in favour of one of the countries by a financial policy directed towards a lowering of its internal price level relatively to the internal price level of the other country. On the other hand a financial policy which has the effect of raising the internal price level must result, sooner or later, in depressing the rate of exchange.

The conclusion is generally drawn, and quite correctly, that budgetary deficits covered by a progressive inflation of the currency render the stabilisation of a country's exchanges impossible; and that the cessation of any increase in the volume of currency, due to this cause, is a necessary prerequisite to a successful attempt at stabilising.

The argument, however, is often carried further than this, and it is supposed that, if a country's budget, currency, foreign trade, and its internal and external price levels are properly adjusted, then, automatically, its foreign exchange will be steady.[1] So long, therefore, as the exchanges fluctuate—thus the argument runs—this in itself is a symptom that an attempt to stabilise would be premature. When, on the other hand, the basic conditions necessary for stabilisation are present, the exchange will steady itself. In short, any deliberate or artificial scheme of stabilisation is attacking the problem at the wrong end. It is the regulation of the currency, by means of sound budgetary and bank-rate policies, that needs attention. The proclamation of convertibility will be the last and crowning stage of the proceedings, and will amount to little more than the announcement of a *fait accompli*.

There is a certain force in this mode of reasoning. But in one important respect it is fallacious.

---

[1] Dr R. Estcourt, criticising one of my articles in *The Annalist* for 12 June 1922, writes: 'The arrangement would not last for any appreciable period unless, as a preliminary, the Governments took the necessary steps to balance their budgets. If that were done, the so-called stabilisation speedily would become unnecessary; exchange would stabilise itself at pre-war rates.' This passage puts boldly an opinion which is widely held.

Even though foreign trade is properly adjusted, and the country's claims and liabilities on foreign account are in equilibrium over the year as a whole, it does not follow that they are in equilibrium every day. Indeed, it is well known that countries which import large quantities of agricultural produce do not find it convenient, if they are to secure just the quality and the amount which they require, to buy at an equal rate throughout the year, but prefer to concentrate their purchases on the autumn period.[1] Thus, quite consistently with equilibrium over the year as a whole, industrial countries tend to owe money to agricultural countries in the second half of the year, and to repay in the first half. The satisfaction of these seasonal requirements for credit with the least possible disturbance to trade was recognised before the war as an important function of international banking, and the seasonal transference of short-term credits from one centre to another was carried out for a moderate commission.

It was possible for this service to be rendered cheaply because, with the certainty provided by convertibility, the price paid for it did not need to include any appreciable provision against risk. A somewhat higher rate of discount in the temporarily debtor country, together with a small exchange profit provided by the

---

[1] Whilst the fact of seasonal pressure is well ascertained, the exact analysis of it is a little complicated. Food arrivals into Great Britain, for example, are nearly 10 per cent heavier in the third and fourth quarters of the year than in the first and second, and reach their maximum in the fourth quarter. (These and the following figures are based on averages for the pre-war period 1901–13 worked out by the Cambridge and London Economic Service.) Raw material imports are more than 20 per cent heavier in the fourth and first quarters than in the second and third, and reach their maximum in the three months November to January. Thus the fourth quarter of the year is the period at which there are heavy imports of both food and raw materials. Manufactured exports, on the other hand, are distributed through the year much more evenly, and are about normal during the last quarter. Allowing for the fact that imports are paid for, generally speaking, before they arrive, these dates correspond pretty closely with the date at which seasonal pressure is actually experienced by the dollar–sterling exchange. In France, since the war, imports in the last quarter of the year seem to have been quite 50 per cent heavier than, for example, in the first quarter. In Italy the third quarter seems to be the slackest, and the last quarter, again, a relatively heavy period. When we turn to the statistics for the United States we find the other side of the picture. August and September are the months of heavy wheat export; October to January those of heavy cotton export. The strength of the dollar exchanges in the early autumn is further increased by the financial pressure in the United States during the crop-moving period, which leads to a withdrawal of funds from foreign centres to New York.

slight shift of the exchanges within the gold points, was quite sufficient.

But what is the position now? As always, the balance of payments must balance every day. As before, the balance of trade is spread unevenly through the year. Formerly the daily balance was adjusted by the movement of bankers' funds, as described above. But now it is no longer a purely bankers' business, suitably and sufficiently rewarded by an arbitrage profit. If a banker moves credits temporarily from one country to another, he cannot be certain at what rate of exchange he will be able to bring them back again later on. Even though he may have a strong opinion as to the probable course of exchange, his profit is no longer definitely calculable beforehand, as it used to be; he has learnt by experience that unforeseen movements of the exchange may involve him in heavy loss; and his prospective profit must be commensurate with the risk he runs. Even if he thinks that the risk is covered actuarially by the prospective profit, a banker cannot afford to run such risks on a large scale. In fact, the seasonal adjustment of credit requirements has ceased to be arbitrage banking business, and demands the services of speculative finance.

Under present conditions, therefore, a large fluctuation of the exchange may be necessary before the daily account can be balanced, even though the annual account is level. Where in the old days a banker would have readily remitted millions to and from New York, hundreds of thousands are now as much as the biggest institutions will risk. The exchange must fall (or rise, as the case may be) until either the speculative financier feels sufficiently confident of a large profit to step in, or the merchant, appalled by the rate of exchange quoted to him for the transaction, decides to forgo the convenience of purchasing at that particular season of the year, and postpones a part of his purchases. The services of the professional exchange speculator, being discouraged by official and banking influences, are generally in short supply, so that a heavy price has to be paid for them, and trade is handicapped by a corresponding expense, in so far as it continues to purchase its materials at the most convenient season of the year.

The extent to which the exchange fluctuations which have troubled trade during the past three years have been seasonal, and therefore due, not to a continuing or increasing disequilibrium, but *merely* to the absence of a fixed exchange, is not, I think, fully appreciated.

During 1919 there was a heavy fall of the chief European exchanges due to the termination of the inter-allied arrangements which had existed during the war. During 1922 there was a rise of the sterling exchange, which was independent of seasonal influences. During 1923 there has been a further non-seasonal collapse of the franc exchange due to certain persisting features of France's internal finances and external policy. But the following table shows how largely *recurrent* the fluctuations have been during the four years since the autumn of 1919:

PERCENTAGE OF DOLLAR PARITY

	Sterling		Francs		Lire	
August–July	Lowest	Highest	Lowest	Highest	Lowest	Highest
1919–20	69	88	31	66	22	56
1920–1	69	82	30	45	18	29
1921–2	73	92	37	48	20	28
1922–3	90	97	29	41	20	27

On the experience of the past three years, francs and lire are at their best in April and May and at their worst between October and December. Sterling is not quite so punctual in its movements, the best point of the year falling somewhere between March and June and the worst between August and November.

The comparative stability of the highest and lowest quotations respectively in each year, especially in the case of Italy, is very striking, and indicates that a policy of stabilisation at some mean figure might have been practicable; whilst, on the other hand,

8-2

the wide divergences between the highest and lowest are a measure of the expense and interference that trade has suffered.

These results correspond so closely to the facts of seasonal trade (see above, p. 89) that we may safely attribute most of the major fluctuations of the exchanges from month to month to the actual pressure of trade remittances, and not to speculation. Speculators, indeed, by anticipating the movements tend to make them occur a little earlier than they would occur otherwise, but by thus spreading the pressure more evenly through the year their influence is to diminish the absolute amount of the fluctuation. General opinion greatly overestimates the influence of exchange speculators acting under the stimulus of merely political and sentimental considerations. Except for brief periods the influence of the speculator is washed out; and political events can only exert a lasting influence on the exchanges, in so far as they modify the internal price level, the volume of trade, or the ability of a country to borrow on foreign markets. A political event, which does not materially affect any of these facts, cannot exert a lasting effect on the exchanges merely by its influence on sentiment. The only important exception to this statement is where there exists on a large scale a long-period speculative investment in a country's currency on the part of foreigners, as in the case of German marks. But such investments are comparable to borrowing abroad and exercise a different kind of influence altogether from a speculative transaction proper, which is opened with the intention of its being closed again within a short period. And even speculative investment in a currency, since it is bound to diminish sooner or later, cannot permanently prevent the exchanges from reaching the equilibrium justified by conditions of trading and relative price levels.

It follows that, whilst purely seasonal fluctuations do not interfere with the forces which determine the ultimate equilibrium of the exchanges, nevertheless stability of the exchange from day to day cannot be maintained merely by the *fact* of stability in these underlying conditions. It is necessary also that bankers should have a sufficiently certain *expectation* of such stability to induce them to look after the daily and seasonal fluctuations of the market in return for a moderate commission.

After recent experience it is unlikely that they will actually entertain any such expectation, even if the underlying facts were of a kind to justify it, with sufficient conviction to act, unless it is backed up by a guarantee on the part of the central authority (bank or government) to employ all their resources for the maintenance of the level of exchange at a stated figure. At present the declared official policy is to bring the franc and the lira (for example) back to par, so that operations favouring a fall of these currencies are not free from danger. On the other hand no steps are taken to make this policy effective, and the conditions of internal finance in France and Italy indicate that their exchanges may go much worse. Thus, since no one can have complete confidence whether they are to be a great deal better or very much worse, there must be a wide fluctuation before financiers will come in, purely from motives of self-interest, to balance the day-to-day fluctuations and the month-to-month fluctuations round about the unpredictable point of equilibrium.

If, therefore, the exchanges are not stabilised by policy, they will never come to an equilibrium of themselves. As time goes on and experience accumulates, the oscillations may be smaller than at present. Speculators may come in a little sooner, and importers may make greater efforts to spread their requirements more evenly over the year. But even so, there must be a substantial difference of rates between the busy season and the slack season, until the business world knows for certain at what level the exchanges in question are going to settle down. Thus a seasonal fluctuation of the exchanges (including the sterling–dollar exchange) is inevitable, even in the absence of any decided long-period tendency of an exchange to rise or to fall, unless the central authority, by a guarantee of convertibility or otherwise, takes special steps to provide against it.

93

4. *The forward market in exchanges*[1]

When a merchant buys or sells goods in a foreign currency the transaction is not always[2] for immediate settlement by cash or negotiable bill. During the interval before he can cover himself by buying or selling (as the case may be) the foreign currency involved, he runs an exchange risk, losses or gains on which may often, in these days, swamp his trading profit. He is thus involuntarily engaged in a heavy risk of a kind which it is hardly in his province to undertake.[3] The subject of what follows is a[4] piece of financial machinery—namely, the market in 'forward' exchanges as distinguished from 'spot' exchanges—for enabling the merchant to avoid this risk, not, indeed, during the interval when he is negotiating the contract, but as soon as[5] the negotiation is completed.

Transactions in 'spot' exchange are for cash—that is to say, cash in one currency is exchanged for cash in another currency. But merchants who have bought goods in terms of foreign currency for future delivery may not have the cash available pending delivery of the goods; whilst merchants who have sold goods in terms of foreign currency, but are not yet in a position to sell a draft on the buyer, cannot, even if they have plenty of cash in their own currency, protect themselves by a 'spot' sale of the exchange involved, save in the exceptional case when they have cash available in the foreign currency also.

A[6] 'forward' contract is for the conclusion of a 'spot' transaction in exchanges at a later date, fixed on the basis of the spot

---

[1] In this section, unless otherwise noted, the text follows the article 'The Forward Market in Foreign Exchanges' of 20 April 1922.

[2] The word 'always' in the text replaces the word 'generally' in the article.

[3] The following additional sentence concludes this paragraph in the article: 'This is the main reason for regarding the chaotic exchanges as partly responsible for the failure of trade to revive.'

[4] In the article, this sentence, which starts a new paragraph, begins 'The object of this article is to discuss a certain'.

[5] The words 'as soon as' in the text replace the word 'immediately' in the article.

[6] In the article, the following sentence precedes the one in the text: 'To meet these difficulties the machinery of the "forward" market is designed.'

rate prevailing at the original date. Pending the date of the maturity of the forward contract no cash need pass (although, of course, the contracting party may be required to give some security or other evidence for his ability to complete the contract in due course), so that the merchant entering into a forward contract is not required to find cash any sooner than if he ran the risk on the exchange until the goods were delivered; yet he is protected from the consequences of any fluctuation in the exchanges in the meantime.

The tables given below show that in London, in the case of the exchanges which have a big market (the dollar, the franc, and the lira),[1] competition between dealers has brought down the charges for these facilities to a fairly moderate rate. During 1920 and 1921[2] the cost to an English buyer of foreign currency for forward delivery was a little more expensive than for spot delivery in the case of francs, lire, and marks, and a little cheaper in the case of dollars. Correspondingly,[3] French, Italian, and German merchants were generally in a position to buy both sterling and dollars for forward delivery at a slightly cheaper rate than for spot delivery—that is to say, if they dealt in London. As regards the rates charged in foreign centres my information is not extensive,[4] but it indicates that in Milan, for example, very much less

[1] In the article, the mark is added to this list.
[2] In the article, this sentence begins 'Generally speaking, during the last two years'.
[3] The word 'correspondingly' in the text replaces the words 'On the other hand' in the article.
[4] In the article, the words 'but I print below some quotations for forward sterling in Milan which indicate that' replace the words 'but...example'. The Milan quotations were as follows:

Discount on forward sterling (or premium on forward lire) over spot, one month forward, in Milan, on the last day of each month:

	Discount on sterling one month forward per £	Equivalent in per cent per annum
1921		
January	1·10 (lire)	12·6
February	2·40	27·2
March	1·50	18·8
April	1·50	22·2

(note continued overleaf)

favourable terms for these transactions are frequently charged to the seller of forward sterling than those ruling in London. During[1] 1922, however, the effect of the progressive cheapening of money in London was, for reasons to be explained in a moment, to cheapen the cost to English buyers of foreign currency for forward delivery, forward francs falling to an appreciable discount on spot francs, and forward dollars becoming at the end of the year decidedly cheaper than spot dollars. Later on, the raising of the bank rate in June 1923 acted again, as could have been predicted, in the opposite direction.

Proceeding to details, we see below (pp. 97–100) the quotations for forward exchange ruling in the London market since the beginning of 1920. During 1920–1[2] forward dollars were generally cheaper than spot dollars to a London buyer to the extent of from 1 to 1½ per cent per annum. Occasionally, however, when big movements of the exchange were taking place, the discount on forward dollars was temporarily much higher, having risen, for example, in November 1920, when sterling was at its lowest point, to nearly 6 per cent—for reasons which I will endeavour to elucidate later. During[3] the first half of 1922 the discount on forward dollars dwindled, but rose again during the latter half of the year, reacting again in the middle of 1923 after

1921 *continued*		
May	0·65	10·2
June	0·80	12·7
July	0·55	7·8
August	0·225	3·2
September	0·21	2·3
October	0·15	1·9
November	0·25	3·1
December	0·35	4·3
1922		
January	0·65	8·1
February	0·60	8·7
March (23)	0·30	4·2

[1] The rest of this paragraph does not appear in the article. Keynes concluded the same paragraph in the article as follows: 'I should be grateful if readers who are in possession of tables showing the rates which have been charged in European centres for forward dealings during the recent past would be good enough to send them to me.'
[2] The words 'during 1920–1...were' in the text replace the words 'it appears that' in the article. [3] This sentence does not appear in the article.

TABLE OF EXCHANGE QUOTATIONS IN
LONDON ONE MONTH FORWARD[1]

Date	New York			Paris		
	Spot	One month forward (cents)	Difference per cent per annum	Spot	One month forward (centimes)	Difference per cent per annum
1920						
January	3.79	$+\frac{3}{8}$	$+1\cdot2$	40.90	$+6$	$+1\cdot7$
February	$3.48\frac{7}{8}$	$+\frac{1}{4}$	$+0\cdot9$	46.90	$+4$	$+1\cdot0$
March	$3.41\frac{3}{8}$	$+\frac{1}{4}$	$+0\cdot9$	48.55	$+3$	$+0\cdot7$
April	$3.90\frac{3}{4}$	$+\frac{3}{8}$	$+1\cdot2$	57.80	$+3$	$+0\cdot6$
May	$3.82\frac{7}{8}$	$+\frac{1}{2}$	$+1\cdot6$	64.04	$+1$	$+0\cdot18$
June	$3.89\frac{15}{16}$	$+\frac{3}{8}$	$+1\cdot2$	50.45	-5	$-1\cdot2$
July	$3.96\frac{1}{8}$	$+\frac{5}{8}$	$+1\cdot9$	47.05	-10	$-2\cdot8$
August	3.67	$+\frac{1}{2}$	$+1\cdot6$	49.00	-10	$-2\cdot4$
September	$3.56\frac{7}{8}$	$+\frac{1}{2}$	$+1\cdot7$	$51.22\frac{1}{2}$	-5	$-1\cdot2$
October	$3.48\frac{5}{16}$	$+\frac{1}{2}$	$+1\cdot7$	52.10	-10	$-2\cdot3$
November	$3.44\frac{3}{8}$	$+1\frac{5}{8}$	$+5\cdot7$	54.45	-15	$-3\cdot3$
December	3.49	$+\frac{1}{2}$	$+1\cdot7$	57.45	-15	$-3\cdot2$
1921						
January	$3.58\frac{3}{8}$	$+\frac{3}{8}$	$+1\cdot3$	$61.07\frac{1}{2}$	-30	$-5\cdot9$
February	$3.84\frac{3}{4}$	$+1$	$+3\cdot1$	54.50	-20	$-4\cdot4$
March	$3.88\frac{3}{8}$	$+\frac{7}{8}$	$+2\cdot7$	54.40	-27	$-5\cdot9$
April	3.92	$+\frac{3}{8}$	$+1\cdot1$	$55.37\frac{1}{2}$	-15	$-3\cdot3$
May	3.98	$+\frac{1}{2}$	$+1\cdot5$	$50.22\frac{1}{2}$	-12	$-2\cdot9$
June	$3.90\frac{5}{8}$	$+\frac{3}{4}$	$+2\cdot3$	46.35	-10	$-2\cdot6$
July	$3.71\frac{15}{16}$	$+\frac{5}{8}$	$+2\cdot0$	$46.72\frac{1}{2}$	-10	$-2\cdot6$
August	$3.56\frac{3}{8}$	$+\frac{1}{2}$	$+1\cdot7$	$46.77\frac{1}{2}$	$+2$	$+0\cdot5$
September	$3.71\frac{5}{8}$	$+\frac{3}{8}$	$+1\cdot2$	$48.68\frac{1}{2}$	$+3$	$+0\cdot7$
October	$3.76\frac{1}{8}$	$+\frac{1}{2}$	$+1\cdot6$	$52.27\frac{1}{2}$	$+1$	$+0\cdot2$
November	$3.92\frac{1}{16}$	$+\frac{7}{8}$	$+2\cdot7$	53.44	$+4$	$+0\cdot9$
December	$4.08\frac{5}{16}$	$+\frac{3}{8}$	$+1\cdot1$	54.24	$+2$	$+0\cdot4$
1922						
January	$4.20\frac{1}{8}$	$+\frac{1}{8}$	$+0\cdot4$	$52.32\frac{1}{2}$	Par	.
February	$4.30\frac{1}{2}$	Par	.	$51.62\frac{1}{2}$	Par	.
March	4.42	Par	.	48.45	Par	.
April	4.39	Par	.	48.15	-1	$-0\cdot25$
May	$4.44\frac{1}{2}$	Par	.	48.47	$+1$	$+0\cdot25$
June	$4.46\frac{3}{4}$	$+\frac{3}{16}$	$+0\cdot5$	49.00	$+2$	$+0\cdot49$
July	$4.44\frac{3}{4}$	$+\frac{1}{16}$	$+0\cdot17$	56.20	$+8$	$+1\cdot8$
August	$4.45\frac{1}{4}$	$+\frac{3}{16}$	$+0\cdot5$	54.10	$+10$	$+2\cdot21$

[1] First day of month in 1920, first Wednesday in 1921, and first Friday thereafter.

TABLE OF EXCHANGE QUOTATIONS IN LONDON
ONE MONTH FORWARD (*continued*)

	New York			Paris		
Date	Spot	One month forward (cents)	Difference per cent per annum	Spot	One month forward (centimes)	Difference per cent per annum
1922 (*continued*)						
September	4.46	$+\frac{3}{8}$	$+1$	57.40	$+3$	$+0\cdot63$
October	4.42	$+\frac{1}{4}$	$+0\cdot68$	58.25	$+3$	$+0\cdot62$
November	4.46$\frac{1}{2}$	$+\frac{5}{8}$	$+1\cdot68$	64.65	$+14$	$+2\cdot59$
December	4.51$\frac{3}{4}$	$+1$	$+2\cdot65$	64.30	$+8$	$+1\cdot49$
1923						
January	4.64$\frac{3}{4}$	$+1\frac{1}{4}$	$+3\cdot23$	66.40	$+5$	$+0\cdot9$
February	4.67	$+\frac{7}{8}$	$+2\cdot25$	75.50	$+16$	$+2\cdot54$
March	4.70$\frac{5}{8}$	$+1$	$+2\cdot55$	77.50	$+11$	$+1\cdot70$
April	4.66$\frac{7}{8}$	$+\frac{3}{4}$	$+1\cdot93$	70.40	$+5$	$+0\cdot85$
May	4.62$\frac{1}{2}$	$+\frac{15}{16}$	$+2\cdot43$	69.35	$+5$	$+0\cdot86$
June	4.62$\frac{3}{4}$	$+\frac{7}{8}$	$+2\cdot27$	71·60	$+5$	$+0\cdot84$
July	4.56$\frac{1}{2}$	$+\frac{1}{2}$	$+1\cdot31$	78.35	$+4$	$+0\cdot61$
August	4.57	$+\frac{1}{4}$	$+0\cdot66$	79.20	$+9$	$+0\cdot60$

money rates in London had been slightly raised. Thus[1] a London merchant, who has had dollar commitments for the purchase of goods, has not only been able to cover his exchange risk by means of a forward transaction, but on the average he has got his exchange a little cheaper by providing for it in advance.

Forward purchases of francs, after being[2] dearer than spot transactions by 2$\frac{1}{2}$ per cent per annum or more[3] from the middle of 1920 to the middle of 1921, were nearly level in price from the middle of 1921 to the middle of 1922, whilst since that time they have been $\frac{1}{2}$ to 2$\frac{1}{2}$ per cent per annum cheaper. In the case of lire there have been much wider gaps,[4] forward purchases

[1] The words 'not only can' appear here in the article replacing the words 'has not only been able' later in the sentence in the text.
[2] The word 'constantly' appears here in the article.
[3] The rest of the sentence in the article runs 'have recently moved nearly level in price or even a little cheaper'.
[4] The words 'have been much wider gaps' in the text replace the words 'is a much wider gap' in the article.

TABLE OF EXCHANGE QUOTATIONS IN LONDON ONE MONTH FORWARD

Date	Italy			Germany		
	Spot	One month forward (lire)	Difference per cent per annum	Spot	One month forward (marks)	Difference per cent per annum
1920[1]						
January	50	$-\frac{1}{8}$	−3·0	187		
February	55	$-\frac{1}{8}$	−2·7	305		
March	$62\frac{3}{4}$	$-\frac{1}{4}$	−4·7	337		
April	$80\frac{1}{2}$	$-\frac{1}{4}$	−3·7	275		
May	83	$-\frac{1}{2}$	−7·1	$218\frac{1}{2}$	−1	−5·5
June	$66\frac{3}{8}$	$-\frac{1}{2}$	−9·1	$150\frac{1}{2}$	−1	−8·0
July	$65\frac{3}{8}$	$-\frac{1}{2}$	−9·2	150	$-\frac{1}{2}$	−4·0
August	70	$-\frac{1}{2}$	−8·5	$160\frac{1}{2}$	−1	−7·5
September	$76\frac{1}{4}$	$-\frac{1}{2}$	−7·9	176	$-\frac{1}{2}$	−3·4
October	$83\frac{9}{16}$	$-\frac{1}{2}$	−7·2	215	−1	−5·6
November	$93\frac{11}{16}$	$-\frac{1}{2}$	−6·4	$266\frac{1}{2}$	$-\frac{1}{2}$	−2·2
December	$94\frac{13}{16}$	$-\frac{1}{2}$	−6·3	$241\frac{1}{2}$	−1	−4·9
1921						
January	$104\frac{3}{8}$	Par	.	$269\frac{1}{2}$	−2	−8·9
February	$105\frac{1}{2}$	$-\frac{3}{4}$	−8·5	$243\frac{1}{2}$	−1	−4·9
March	$106\frac{1}{2}$	$-\frac{5}{8}$	−7·0	$243\frac{3}{4}$	−1	−4·9
April	$92\frac{1}{4}$	$-\frac{1}{2}$	−6·5	$239\frac{1}{2}$	−2	−10·0
May	$81\frac{3}{8}$	$-\frac{5}{8}$	−9·1	$262\frac{1}{2}$	$-1\frac{3}{4}$	−8·0
June	$73\frac{11}{16}$	$-\frac{1}{2}$	−8·1	$245\frac{1}{4}$	$-1\frac{1}{2}$	−7·3
July	77	$-\frac{1}{2}$	−7·8	$279\frac{1}{2}$	$-1\frac{1}{2}$	−6·45
August	$85\frac{1}{16}$	$-\frac{1}{4}$	−3·5	286	−1	−4·2
September	$85\frac{9}{16}$	$-\frac{3}{8}$	−5·2	$347\frac{1}{2}$	$-1\frac{1}{2}$	−5·1
October	$94\frac{1}{8}$	$-\frac{3}{8}$	−4·8	471	−5	−12·7
November	$96\frac{5}{8}$	$-\frac{1}{4}$	−3·1	$764\frac{1}{2}$	$-2\frac{1}{4}$	−3·5
December	$93\frac{15}{16}$	$-\frac{1}{2}$	−6·4	855	$-1\frac{1}{2}$	−2·1
1922						
January	$97\frac{1}{8}$	$-\frac{1}{4}$	−3·0	$777\frac{1}{2}$	$-3\frac{1}{2}$	−5·4
February	$92\frac{1}{2}$	$-\frac{7}{16}$	−5·7	872	$-2\frac{1}{2}$	−3·4
March	$83\frac{3}{16}$	$-\frac{1}{4}$ (points)	−3·6	1,117	$-1\frac{1}{2}$	−1·6
April	$83\frac{5}{16}$	−15	−2·16	1,440	−8	−6·6
May	83	−10	−1·45	1,270	$-\frac{1}{2}$	−0·47
June	$85\frac{7}{8}$	−3	−0·41	1,222	Par	.
July	100	Par	.	2,320	+5	−2·59
August	96	Par	.	3,175	+20	−7·56
September	101	−11	−1·31	5,700	nominal	.
October	103	−10	−1·16	9,900	+450	+54·54
November	106	−8	−0·91	26,250	+6,000	+274·3
December	$93\frac{3}{4}$	−20	−2·56	35,000	+5,500	+188·58

[1] Nominal.

99

TABLE OF EXCHANGE QUOTATIONS IN LONDON
ONE MONTH FORWARD (*continued*)

Date	Italy			Germany		
	Spot	One month forward (lire)	Difference per cent per annum	Spot	One month forward (marks)	Difference per cent per annum
1923						
January	92	− 11	− 1·43	39,500	+ 1,750	+ 53·16
February	97½	− 23	− 2·83	190,000	+ 27,000	+ 170·53
March	97⅜	− 23	− 2·82	105,000	+ 10,000	+ 114·28
April	93¾	− 18	− 2·30	97,500	+ 60,000	+ 73·85
May	94⅞	− 19	− 2·28	170,000	+ 20,000	+ 141·18
June	99	− 15	− 1·82	350,000	+ 40,000	+ 137·14
July	106⅞	− 22	− 2·47	900,000	+ 30,000[1]	+ 40·00
August	105½	− 28	− 3·18	5,500,000	+ 1,500,000[1]	+ 327·27

being frequently[1] 3 per cent or more dearer than spot. In[2] the case of German marks, the forward rate, after ranging round about 5 per cent per annum dearer than spot, has reached, since the autumn of 1922 and the complete collapse of the mark, a figure fantastically cheaper, thus reflecting the sensational rate of interest for short loans current inside Germany.

But in all these cases (except in Germany since the complete collapse of the mark),[3] whether forward exchange is at a discount or at a premium on spot, the expense, if any, of dealing forward has been[4] small in relation to the risks that are avoided.

Nevertheless,[5] in practice merchants do not avail themselves of these facilities to the extent that might have been expected. The nature of forward dealings in exchange is not generally understood. The rates are seldom quoted in the newspapers.

---

[1] The rest of the sentence in the article runs 'round 6 per cent per annum dearer than spot, though the difference has narrowed recently'.

[2] This sentence in the article runs as follows: 'In the case of German marks, after a period of wide differences, forward purchases have narrowed lately to a cost of 5 per cent per annum or less above spot.'

[3] The material in parentheses does not appear in the article.

[4] The words 'has been' in the text replace the word 'is' in the article.

[5] At this point in the article the words 'enquiry seems to show that' are added.

There are few financial topics of equal importance which have received so little discussion or publicity. The present situation did not exist before the war (although even at that time forward rates for the dollar were regularly quoted),[1] and did not begin until after the 'unpegging' of the leading exchanges in 1919, so that the business world has[2] only begun to adapt itself. Moreover, for the ordinary man,[3] dealing in forward exchange has, it seems,[4] a smack of speculation about it. Unlike Manchester cotton spinners, who have learnt by long experience that it is not the hedging of open cotton commitments on the Liverpool futures market, but the failure to do so, which is speculative, merchants, who buy or sell goods of which the price is expressed in a foreign currency, do not yet regard it as part of the normal routine of prudent business to hedge these indirect exchange commitments by a transaction in forward exchange.

It is important, on the other hand, not to exaggerate the extent to which, at the present time, merchants can by this means protect themselves from risk. In the first place, for reasons, some of which will be considered below, it is only in certain of the leading exchanges that these transactions can be carried out at a reasonable charge.[5] It is not clear that even the banks themselves have yet learnt to look on the provision for their clients of such facilities at fair and reasonable rates as one of the most useful services they can offer. They have been too much influenced, perhaps,

[1] The words in parentheses in the text run as follows in the article: 'although it is true that forward rates for the dollar were already quoted at that time'.

[2] The rest of this sentence runs in the article 'had barely two years in which to adapt itself'.

[3] The word 'man' in the text replaces the word 'mind' in the article.

[4] The words 'it seems' do not appear in the article.

[5] In the article, the rest of this paragraph runs as follows: 'Here again I should be grateful for precise information from those who have it. For example, I have not yet obtained detailed tables of the rates for forward dealings in the Indian rupee, but the available information indicates that the rates quoted by the Eastern banks for forward purchases of rupees range up to the equivalent of as much as 12 per cent per annum, without there being any apparent excuse for so high a charge—unless it be that, the bulk of the business being done in India, the London market is too small for close rates to rule in it. It is not clear that even the banks themselves have yet learnt to look on the provision for their clients of such facilities at fair and reasonable rates as one of the most useful services they can offer. They have been too much influenced, perhaps, by the fear that these facilities might tend at the same time to increase speculation.'

by the fear that these facilities might tend at the same time to increase speculation.

But there is a further qualification, not to be overlooked, to the value of forward transactions as a protection against risk. The price of a particular commodity,[1] in terms of a particular currency, does[2] not exactly respond to changes in the value of that currency on the exchange markets of the world, with the result that a movement in a country's exchanges may, in the case of a commodity of which that country is a large seller or a large purchaser, change the commodity's world value expressed in terms of gold. In that case a merchant, even though he is hedged in respect of the exchange itself, may lose, in respect of his unsold trading stocks, through a movement in the world value of the commodity he is dealing in, directly occasioned by the exchange fluctuation.

If[3] we turn to the theoretical analysis of the forward market, what is it that determines the amount and the sign (whether plus or minus) of the divergence between the spot and forward rates as recorded above?

If dollars one month forward are quoted cheaper than spot dollars to a London buyer in terms of sterling, this indicates a preference by the market, on balance, in favour of holding funds in New York during the month in question rather than in London—a preference the degree of which is measured by the discount on forward dollars. For if spot dollars are worth $4.40 to the pound and dollars one month forward $4.40½ to the pound, then the owner of $4.40 can, by selling the dollars spot and buying them back one month forward, find himself at the end of the month with $4.40½, merely by being during the month

[1] In the article, the sentence to this point runs 'The prices of commodities'.
[2] The word 'does' in the text replaces the word 'do' in the article.
[3] In the article, this paragraph is replaced by the following:

'WHAT FIXES FORWARD RATES?

Let readers, who are not interested in the theoretical basis of the futures market, stop here and avoid the following analysis of the factors which determine the amount and the sign (whether plus or minus) of the divergence between the spot and forward rates.'

the owner of £1 in London instead of $4.40 in New York. That he should require and can obtain half a cent, which, earned in one month, is equal to about $1\frac{1}{2}$ per cent per annum, to induce him to do the transaction, shows, and is, under conditions of competition, a measure of the market's preference for holding funds during the month in question in New York rather than in London.

Conversely, if francs, lire, and marks one month forward are quoted dearer than the spot rates to a London buyer, this indicates a preference for holding funds in London rather than in Paris, Rome, or Berlin.

The[1] difference between the spot and forward rates is, therefore, precisely and exactly the measure of the preference of the money and exchange market for holding funds in one international centre rather than in another, *the exchange risk apart*, that is to say under conditions in which the exchange risk is covered. What is it that determines these preferences?

1. The most fundamental cause is to be found in the interest[2] rates obtainable on 'short' money—that is to say, on money lent or deposited for short periods of time in the money markets of the two centres under comparison. If by lending dollars in New York for one month the lender could earn interest at the rate of $5\frac{1}{2}$ per cent per annum, whereas by lending sterling in London for one month he could only earn interest at the rate of 4 per cent, then the preference observed above for holding funds in New York rather than in London is wholly explained. That is to say, forward quotations for the purchase of the currency of the dearer money market tend to be cheaper than spot quotations by a percentage per month equal to[3] the excess of the interest which can be earned in a month in the dearer market over what

[1] In the article, this paragraph runs as follows (The phrase 'the table below' referring to an earlier version of pages 97–100): 'The measures of these preferences at different dates since the beginning of the year 1920 are given in the table printed below. What is the explanation of them?'

[2] The word 'interest' does not appear in the article.

[3] The words 'be cheaper than spot quotations by a percentage per month equal to' in the text replace the words 'stand at a discount on spot quotations to an extent per month measured by' in the article.

can be earned in the cheaper. It must be noticed that the governing factor is the rate of interest obtainable for short periods, so that a country where, owing to the absence or ill-development of an organised money market, it is difficult to lend money satisfactorily at call or for very short periods, may, for the purposes of this calculation, reckon as a low interest-earning market, even though the prevailing rate of interest for longer periods is not low at all. This consideration generally tends to make London and New York more attractive markets for short money than any Continental centres.

The[1] effect of the cheap money rates ruling in London from the middle of 1922 to the middle of 1923 in diminishing the attractiveness of London as a depository of funds is strikingly shown, in the above tables, by the cheapening of the forward quotations of foreign currencies relatively to the spot quotations. In the case of the dollar the forward quotation had risen by the beginning of 1923 to a rate 3 per cent per annum above the spot quotation (i.e. forward dollars were 3 per cent per annum *cheaper* than spot dollars in terms of sterling), which meant (subject to modification by the other influences to be mentioned below) that the effective rate for short loans approached 3 per cent higher in New York than in London.

In the case of francs forward quotations which had been below spot, so long as money was dear in London, rose above the spot quotations, thus indicating that the relative dearness of money in London as compared with Paris had disappeared; whilst in the case of lire forward quotations, although still below spot quotations, rose, under the same influence, nearer to the spot level. Nevertheless, in the case of both these currencies, a preponderance of bearish anticipations about their future prospects probably also played a part, for the reasons given in detail below, in producing the observed result.

The most interesting figures, however, are those relating to marks, which illustrate vividly what I have mentioned on page 22

---

[1] The next three paragraphs do not appear in the article.

above concerning the enormous money rates of interest current in Germany subsequent to the collapse of October 1922, as a result of the effort of the real rate of interest to remain positive in face of a general anticipation of a catastrophic collapse of the monetary unit. It will be noticed that the effective short money rate of interest in terms of marks ranged from 50 per cent per annum upwards, until finally the quotations were merely nominal.

2. If questions of credit did not enter in, the factor of the rate of interest on short loans[1] would be the dominating one. Indeed, as between London and New York, it probably is so under existing conditions. Between London and Paris it is still important. But elsewhere the various uncertainties of financial and political risk, which the war has left behind, introduce a further element which sometimes quite transcends the factor of relative interest. The possibility of financial trouble or political disturbance, and the quite appreciable probability of a moratorium in the event of any difficulties arising, or of the sudden introduction of exchange regulations which would interfere with the movement of balances out of the country, and even sometimes the contingency of a drastic demonetisation—all these factors deter bankers, even when the exchange risk proper is eliminated, from maintaining large floating balances at certain foreign centres. Such risks prevent the business from being based, as it should be, on a mathematical calculation of interest rates; they obliterate by their possible magnitude the small 'turns' which can be earned out of differences between interest rates plus a normal banker's commission; and, being incalculable, they may even deter conservative bankers from doing the business on a substantial scale at any reasonable rate at all. In[2] the case of Roumania or Poland, for example, this factor is, at times, the dominating one.

3. There is a third factor of some significance. We have assumed so far that the forward rate is fixed at such a level that the

---

[1] The words 'the factor of the rate of interest on short loans' in the text replace the words 'the above factor' in the article.

[2] This sentence does not appear in the article.

dealer or banker can cover himself by a simultaneous spot transaction and be left with a reasonable profit for his trouble But it is not necessary to cover every forward transaction by a corresponding spot transaction; it may be possible to 'marry' a forward sale with a forward purchase of the same currency. For example, whilst some of the market's clients may wish to sell forward dollars, other clients will wish to buy forward dollars. In this case the market can set off these, one against the other, in its books, and there will be no need of any movement of cash funds in either direction. The third factor depends, therefore, on whether it is the sellers or the buyers of forward dollars who predominate. To fix our minds, let us suppose that money-market conditions exist in which a sale of forward dollars against the purchase of spot dollars, at a discount of $1\frac{1}{2}$ per cent per annum for the former, yields neither profit nor loss. Now if in these conditions the purchasers of forward dollars, other than arbitragers, exceed sellers of forward[1] dollars, then this excess of demand for forward dollars can be met by arbitragers, who have cash resources in London, at a discount which falls short of $1\frac{1}{2}$ per cent per annum by such amount (say $\frac{1}{2}$ per cent) as will yield the arbitragers sufficient profit for their trouble. If, however, sellers of forward[1] dollars exceed the purchasers, then a sufficient discount has to be accepted by the former to induce arbitrage the other way round—that is to say, by arbitragers who have cash resources in New York—namely, a discount which exceeds $1\frac{1}{2}$ per cent per annum by, say, $\frac{1}{2}$ per cent. Thus the discount on forward dollars will fluctuate between 1 and 2 per cent per annum according as buyers or sellers predominate.

4. Lastly, we have to provide for the case, quite frequent in practice, where our assumption of a large and free market breaks down. A business in forward exchange can only be transacted by banks or similar institutions. If the bulk of the business in a particular exchange is in a few hands, or if there is a tacit agreement between the principal institutions concerned to main-

[1] The word 'forward' in the text replaces the word 'future' in the article.

tain differences which will allow more than a competitive profit, then the surcharge representing the profit of a bank for arbitraging between spot and forward transactions may much exceed the moderate figure indicated above.[1] The quotations[2] of the rates charged in Milan for forward dealings in lire, when compared with the rates current in London at the same date, indicate that a bank which is free to operate in both markets can frequently make an abnormal profit.

But there is a further contingency of considerable importance which occurs when speculation is exceptionally active and is all one way. It must be remembered that the floating capital normally available, and ready to move from centre to centre for the purpose of taking advantage of moderate arbitrage profits between spot and forward exchange, is by no means unlimited in amount, and is not always adequate to the market's requirements. When, for example, the market is feeling unusually bullish of the European exchanges as against sterling, or of sterling as against dollars, the pressure to sell forward sterling or dollars, as the case may be, may drive the forward price of these currencies to a discount on their spot price which represents an altogether abnormal profit to anyone who is in a position to buy these currencies forward and sell them spot. This abnormal discount can only disappear when[3] the high profit of arbitrage[4] between spot and forward has drawn[5] fresh capital into the arbitrage business. So few persons understand even the elements of the theory of the forward exchanges that there was an occasion in 1920,[6] even between

---

[1] At this point in the article, the following sentence appears: 'If, for example, the rates mentioned above as being charged by the Eastern banks for forward transactions in the Indian rupee are accurate, this would seem to show that conditions of effective competition do not prevail.'

[2] At this point in the article, the words 'given below' appear. The quotations referred to appear on page 95.

[3] The words 'only disappear when' in the text replace the words 'only be cured by' in the article.

[4] The words 'of arbitrage' in the text replace the words 'which it brings to an arbitrager' in the article.

[5] The words 'has drawn' in the text replace the word 'drawing' in the article.

[6] The words 'was an occasion in 1920' in the text replace the words 'have been occasions in recent times' in the article.

London and New York, when a seller of spot dollars could earn at the rate of 6 per cent per annum above the London rate for short money[1] by converting his dollars into sterling and providing at the same time by a forward sale of the sterling for reconversion into dollars in a month's time; whilst, according to figures supplied me,[2] it was possible, at the end of February 1921, by selling spot sterling in Milan and buying it back a month forward, to earn at the rate of more than 25 per cent per annum over and above any interest obtainable on a month's deposit of cash lire in Milan.

It is interesting to notice that when[3] the differences between forward and spot rates have become temporarily abnormal, thus indicating an exceptional pressure of speculative activity, the speculators have often turned out to be right. For example, the abnormal discount on forward dollars, which persisted more or less from November 1920 to February 1921, thus indicating that the market was a bull of sterling, coincided with the sensational rise of sterling from 3.45 to 3.90. This discount was at its maximum when sterling touched its lowest point and at its minimum (in the middle of[4] May 1921) when sterling reached its highest point on that swing, which showed a remarkably accurate anticipation of events by the balance of professional opinion. The[5] comparatively high discount on forward dollars current at the end of 1922 may, in the same way, have been partly due to an excess of bull speculation in favour of sterling based on an expectation of its recovery towards par, and not merely to the cheapness of money in London as compared with New York.

[1] The words running between 'by' and 'time' in the text replace the words 'by transferring his dollars to London and leaving them there a month' in the article.
[2] The words 'and printed below' are added here in the article. The figures referred to appear on page 95.
[3] The words 'to notice that when' in the text replace the words 'to discover from a study of the tables printed below that on occasions on which'. The tables referred to appear on pages 97–100.
[4] In the article, the words 'the middle of' do not appear.
[5] In the article, this sentence is replaced by the following: 'That forward dollars should have been practically at par with spot during February and March of this year indicates, having regard to current money-market conditions, that this same opinion feels that sterling has gone quite high enough for the time being.'

The[1] same thing seems to have been true for the franc. In January and February 1921, the abnormal premium on the forward franc indicated that, in the view of the market, the franc had fallen too low, which turned out to be the case. They turned round at the precise moment when the franc reached its highest value (end of July 1921), and were right again. During[2] the first five months of 1922, when the franc was almost stable, spot and forward quotations were practically at par with one another, whilst the progressive fall of the franc since June 1922 has been accompanied by a steady and sometimes substantial discount on forward francs; indicating, on this test, that the professional market was bearish of francs and therefore right once more. The lira tells somewhat[3] the same tale. Thus, whilst the reader can see for himself by a study of the tables[4] that no precise generalisation would be accurate, nevertheless the market has been broadly right when it has taken a very decided view, as measured by forward rates.

This result may seem surprising in view of the huge amounts which exchange speculators in European currencies, more particularly on the bull side, are reputed to have lost. But the mass of amateur speculators throughout the world operate by cash purchases of the currency of which they are bulls, forward transactions being neither known nor available to them. Such speculation may afford temporary support to the spot exchange, but it has no influence on the difference between spot and forward, the subject now under discussion. The above conclusion is limited to the fact that when the type of professional speculation which makes use of the forward market is exceptionally active and united in its opinion, it has proved roughly correct, and has, therefore, been a useful factor in moderating the extreme fluctuations which would have occurred otherwise.

[1] In the article, this sentence is replace by the following: 'The same phenomenon is shown by the table for the franc.'
[2] This sentence does not appear in the article.
[3] The word 'somewhat' does not appear in the article.
[4] In the article, the words 'given below' are added here. The tables referred to appear on pages 97-100.

Out[1] of the various practical conclusions which might be drawn from this discussion and the figures which accompany it, I will pick out three.

1. Those[2] exchanges in which the fluctuations are wildest and the merchant is most in need of facilities for hedging his risk are precisely those in which facilities for forward dealing at moderate rates are least developed. But this is to be explained, not necessarily[3] by the instability of the exchange in itself, but by certain accompanying circumstances, such as distrust of the country's internal arrangements or its banking credit, a fear of the sudden imposition of exchange regulations or of a moratorium, and the other analogous influences mentioned above (p. 105). There is no theoretical reason why there should not be an excellent forward market in a highly unstable exchange. In those countries, therefore, where regulation is still premature,[4] it may nevertheless be possible to mitigate the evil consequences of fluctuation by organising facilities for forward dealings.

This is a function which[5] the state banks of such countries could usefully perform. For this[6] they must either themselves command a certain amount of foreign currency or they must provide facilities for accepting short-period deposits in their own currency from foreign bankers, on conditions which inspire these bankers with complete confidence in the freedom and liquidity of such deposits. Various technical devices could be suggested. But[7] the simplest method might be for the state banks themselves

---

[1] In the article, this paragraph is replaced by the following:

'PRACTICAL CONCLUSIONS

Perhaps there are a good many practical conclusions which might be drawn from this discussion and the figures which accompany it. But I will pick out three.'

[2] In the article, the word 'those' follows the words 'It is noticeable that'.

[3] The word 'necessarily' does not appear in the article.

[4] The words 'where regulation is still premature' in the text replace the words 'where an attempt to stabilise the exchange on the lines of my first article above is still premature' in the article. The article referred to is 'The Stabilisation of the European Exchanges: A Plan for Genoa', *Manchester Guardian Commercial, Reconstruction in Europe*, 20 April 1922. This article is reprinted in volume xix.

[5] The words 'in my judgment' appear here in the article.

[6] The words 'for this' in the text replace the words 'to effect this' in the article.

[7] The words 'I think' appear here in the article.

to enter the forward market and offer to buy or sell forward exchange at a reasonable discount or premium on the spot quotation. I suggest that they should deal not direct with the public but only with approved banks and financial houses, from whom they should require adequate security; that they should quote every day their rates for buying and selling exchange either one or three months forward; but that such quotation should take the form, not of a price for the exchange itself, but of a percentage difference between spot and forward, and should be a quotation for the double transaction of a spot deal one way and a simultaneous forward deal the other—e.g. the Bank of Italy might offer to sell spot sterling and buy forward sterling at a premium of $\frac{1}{8}$ per cent per month for the former over the latter, and to buy spot sterling and sell forward sterling at par. For the transaction of such business the state banks would require to command a certain amount of resources abroad, either in cash or in borrowing facilities. But this fund would be a revolving one, automatically replenished at the maturity of the forward contracts, so that it need not be on anything like the scale necessary for a fund for the purpose of supporting the exchange. Nor is it a business which involves any more risk than is inherent in all banking business as such; from exchange risk proper it is free.[1]

With free forward markets thus established no merchant need run an exchange risk unless he wishes[2] to, and business might find a stable foothold even in a fluctuating world.[3] A recommendation in favour of action along these lines was included

[1] The following sentences appear after this point in the article: 'Indeed, I fancy that European state banks would not find it difficult to find British banks who would be glad to act as their correspondents for this purpose and to lend them money for one- and three-monthly periods against their general credit and their holding of contracts for forward sterling.

'In the case of Austria, for example, one of the first purposes to which, if I had any responsibility for their finances, I should put a part of the foreign resources lately made available to them by the Powers, would be the establishment of a free forward market for the krone on the above lines.

'And in the case of Roumania, I should hasten to abolish all exchange regulations whatever and provide a forward market for the leu.'

[2] The word 'wishes' in the text is past tense in the article.

[3] The rest of this paragraph and the next paragraph do not appear in the article.

amongst the financial resolutions of the Genoa Conference of 1922.

I shall develop below (chapter 5) a proposal that the Bank of England should strengthen its control by fixing spot and forward prices for gold every Thursday just as it now fixes its discount rate. But other central banks also would increase their control over fluctuations in exchange if they were to adopt the above plan of quoting rates for forward exchange in terms of spot exchange. By varying these rates they would be able, in effect, to vary the interest offered for *foreign* balances, as a policy distinct from whatever might be their bank-rate policy for the purpose of governing the interest obtainable on *home* balances.

2. It is not unusual at present for banks to endeavour to distinguish between speculative dealings in forward exchange and dealings which are intended to hedge a commercial transaction, with a view to discouraging the former; whilst official exchange regulations in many countries have been aimed at such discrimination. I think that this is a mistake. Banks should take stringent precautions to make sure that their clients are in a position to meet any losses which may accrue without serious[1] embarrassment. But, having fully assured themselves on this point, it is not useful that they should enquire further—for the following reasons.

In the first place, it is almost impossible to prevent the evasion of such regulations; whilst, if the business is[2] driven to methods of evasion, it[3] tends to be pressed underground, to yield excessive profits to middlemen, and to fall into undesirable hands.

But, what is more important and is less appreciated, the speculator with resources can provide a useful, indeed almost an essential, service. Since the volume of actual trade is spread unevenly through the year, the seasonal fluctuation, as explained

[1] The word 'serious' in the text replaces the word 'excessive' in the article.
[2] The words 'whilst if the business is' in the text replace the words 'whereas by being' in the article.
[3] The word 'it' in the text replaces the words 'the whole business' in the article.

above,[1] is bound to occur with undue force unless some financial, non-commercial factor steps in to balance matters.[2] A free
forward market,[3] from which speculative transactions are not
excluded, will give by far the best facilities for the trader, who
does not wish to speculate, to avoid doing so. The same sort of
advantages will be secured for merchants generally as are afforded,
for example, to the cotton trade by the dealings in 'futures' in
the New York and Liverpool markets. Where risk is unavoidably
present, it is much better that it should be carried by those who
are qualified or are desirous[4] to bear it, than by traders, who
have neither the qualification nor the desire to do so, and whose
minds it distracts from their own business. The wide fluctuations
in the leading exchanges over the past three[5] years, as distinct
from their persisting depreciation, have been due,[6] not to the
presence of speculation, but to the absence of a sufficient volume
of it relatively to the volume of trade.[7]

3. A failure to analyse the relation between spot and forward
exchange may be, sometimes,[8] partly responsible for a mistaken
bank-rate policy.[9] Dear money—that is to say, high interest rates
for short-period loans—has two effects.[10] The one is indirect and

---

[1] The words 'as explained above' in the text replace the words 'which is emphasised and lamented by more than one of the writers of the following articles' in the article.
[2] The following additional sentence appeared in the article at this point: 'When exchanges are "pegged" the business of spreading remittance through the year can be safely undertaken by bankers for a moderate "turn"; but when exchanges are not stabilised, a risk is involved which it is unsuitable for banks to carry on a large scale, so that, if speculators are excluded or discouraged, the supply of the service of what economists call "risk bearing" may be inadequate, and the price charged by those, who do in the end carry it, may be unnecessarily large.'
[3] The word 'market' in the text replaces the word 'movement' in the article.
[4] The word 'desirous' in the text replaces the word 'anxious' in the article.
[5] The word 'three' in the text replaces the word 'two' in the article.
[6] The words 'in my judgment' are added here in the article.
[7] The following additional sentence concluded this paragraph in the article: 'I differ, therefore, from Dr Giannini's judgment, expressed in his article below, as to the detrimental effect of professional speculation on the lira exchange (although agreeing with him in many other particulars).'
The article referred to is 'The Lira Exchange, with Special Reference to Seasonal Fluctuation', *Manchester Guardian Commercial, Reconstruction in Europe*, 20 April 1922.
[8] The words 'may be, sometimes,' in the text replace the word 'is' in the article.
[9] The words 'a mistaken bank-rate policy' in the text replace the words 'mistaken policies of bank rate' in the article.
[10] The word 'effects' in the text replaces the word 'results' in the article.

gradual—namely,[1] in diminishing the volume of credit quoted by the banks. This effect is much the same now as it always was. It is desirable to produce it when prices are rising and business is trying to expand faster than the supply of real capital and effective demand can permit in the long run. It is undesirable when prices are falling and trade is depressed.

The other effect of dear money, or rather of dearer money in one centre than in another, used to be to draw gold from the cheaper centre for temporary employment in the dearer. But nowadays the only immediate effect is to cause a new adjustment of the difference between the spot and forward rates of exchange between the two centres. If money becomes dearer in London, the discount on forward dollars diminishes or gives way to a premium. The[2] effect has been pointed out above of the relative cheapening of money in London in the latter half of 1922 in increasing the discount on forward dollars, and of the relative raising of money rates in the middle of 1923 in diminishing the discount. Such are,[3] in present circumstances, the principal direct consequences[4] of a moderate difference between interest rates in the two centres, apart, of course, from the indirect, long-period influence. Since no one is likely to remit money temporarily from one money market to another on any important scale, with an uncovered exchange risk, merely to take advantage of $\frac{1}{2}$ or 1 per cent per annum difference in the interest rate, the direct effect of dearer money on the *absolute*[5] level of the exchanges, as distinguished from the difference between spot and forward,[6] is very small, being limited to the comparatively slight influence which the relation between spot and forward rates exerts on

[1] The rest of this sentence in the article runs: 'the effect in discouraging expansion in the trade of the country as a whole by raising one element of cost, in increasing the expense of carrying stocks of every kind, and in reacting on the long-period rate of interest and so on the prices of securities generally'.
[2] This sentence does not appear in the article.
[3] The words 'such are' in the text replace the words 'this is' in the article.
[4] The words 'the principal direct consequences' in the text replace the words 'the only significant consequence' in the article.
[5] In the article, the word 'absolute' is not italicised.
[6] In the article, the rest of this sentence runs 'is practically nil'.

exchange speculators.[1] The pressure of arbitragers between spot and forward exchange, seeking to take advantage of the new situation, leads to a rapid adjustment of the difference between these rates, until the business of temporary remittance, as distinct from exchange speculation,[2] is no more profitable than it was before, and consequently does not occur on any increased scale; with the result that there is no marked effect on the absolute level of the spot rate.

The[3] reasons given for the maintenance of a close relationship between the Bank of England's rate and that of the American Federal Reserve Board sometimes show confusion. The eventual influence of an effective high bank rate on the general situation is undisputed; but the belief that a moderate difference between bank rates in London and New York reacts directly on the sterling–dollar exchange, as it used to do under a régime of convertibility, is a misapprehension. The direct reaction of this difference is on the discount for forward dollars as against spot dollars; and it cannot much affect the absolute level of the spot rate unless the change in relative money rates is comparable in magnitude (as it used to be but no longer is) with the possible range of exchange fluctuations.

[1] [If interest rates are raised in London, the discount on forward dollars will decrease or a premium will appear. This is likely to have some influence in encouraging speculative sales of forward dollars (how much influence depends on the proportion borne by the difference between the spot and forward rates to the probable range of fluctuation of the spot rate which the speculator anticipates); and in so far as this is the case, the covering sales of spot dollars by banks will move the rate of exchange in favour of London.]

[2] In the article, the words 'as distinct from exchange speculation' do not appear.

[3] The last paragraph of the article runs as follows:
'The reasons sometimes given for the maintenance in London of a Bank rate, which for times of acute depression is still high, especially the alleged necessity of a close relationship between the Bank of England's rate and that of the American Federal Reserve Board, seem to indicate a deep-seated mental confusion. The eventual influence of an effective high Bank rate on the general situation is undisputed; but the belief that a moderate difference between bank rates in London and New York reacts directly on the sterling–dollar exchange is a misapprehension. The direct reaction of this difference is on the discount for forward dollars.'

Chapter 4

ALTERNATIVE AIMS IN
MONETARY POLICY

Our first two chapters, on the evils proceeding from instability in the purchasing power of money and on the part played by the exigencies of public finance, have indicated the practical importance of our subject to the welfare of society. In the third chapter an attempt has been made to lay a foundation of theory upon which to raise constructions. We can now turn, in this and the following chapter, to *remedies*.

The instability of money has been compounded, in most countries except the United States, of two elements: the failure of the national currencies to remain stable in terms of what was supposed to be the standard of value, namely gold; and the failure of gold itself to remain stable in terms of purchasing power. Attention has been mainly concentrated (e.g. by the Cunliffe Committee) on the first of these two factors. It is often assumed that the restoration of the gold standard, that is to say, of the convertibility of each national currency at a fixed rate in terms of gold, must be, in any case, our objective; and that the main question of controversy is whether national currencies should be restored to their pre-war gold value or to some lower value nearer to the present facts; in other words, the choice between *deflation* and *devaluation*.

This assumption is hasty. If we glance at the course of prices during the last five years, it is obvious that the United States, which has enjoyed a gold standard throughout, has suffered as severely as many other countries, that in the United Kingdom the instability of gold has been a larger factor than the instability of the exchange, that the same is true even of France, and that in Italy it has been nearly as large. On the other hand, in India, which has suffered violent exchange fluctuations, the standard of value, as we shall see below, has been more stable than in any other country.

We should not, therefore, by fixing the exchanges get rid of our currency troubles. It is even possible that this step might weaken our control. The problem of stabilisation has several sides, which we must consider one by one:

1. Devaluation *versus* deflation. Do we wish to fix the standard of value, whether or not it be gold, near the existing value? Or do we wish to restore it to the pre-war value?

2. Stability of prices *versus* stability of exchange. Is it more important that the value of a national currency should be stable in terms of purchasing power, or stable in terms of the currency of certain foreign countries?

3. The restoration of a gold standard. In the light of our answers to the first two questions, is a gold standard, however imperfect in theory, the best available method for attaining our ends in practice?

Having decided between these alternative aims, we can proceed, in the next chapter, to some constructive suggestions.

1. *Devaluation* versus *deflation*

The policy of reducing the ratio between the volume of a country's currency and its requirements of purchasing power in the form of money, so as to increase the exchange value of the currency in terms of gold or of commodities, is conveniently called *deflation*.

The alternative policy of stabilising the value of the currency somewhere near its present value, without regard to its pre-war value, is called *devaluation*.

Up to the date of the Genoa Conference of April 1922, these two policies were not clearly distinguished by the public, and the sharp opposition between them has been only gradually appreciated. Even now (October 1923) there is scarcely any European country in which the authorities have made it clear whether their policy is to stabilise the value of their currency or to raise it.

Stabilisation at the existing level has been recommended by International Conferences;[1] and the actual value of many currencies tends to fall rather than to rise. But, to judge from other indications, the heart's desire of the state banks of Europe, whether they pursue it successfully, as in Czechoslovakia, or unusccessfully, as in France, is to *raise* the value of their currencies. In only one country so far have practical steps been taken to *fix* the exchange, namely in Austria.

The simple arguments against deflation fall under two heads.

In the first place, deflation is not *desirable*, because it effects, what is always harmful, a change in the existing standard of value, and redistributes wealth in a manner injurious, at the same time, to business and to social stability. Deflation, as we have already seen, involves a transference of wealth from the rest of the community to the *rentier* class and to all holders of titles to money; just as inflation involves the opposite. In particular it involves a transference from all borrowers, that is to say from traders, manufacturers, and farmers, to lenders, from the active to the inactive.

But whilst the oppression of the taxpayer for the enrichment of the *rentier* is the chief lasting result, there is another, more violent, disturbance during the period of transition. The policy of gradually raising the value of a country's money to (say) 100 per cent above its present value in terms of goods—I repeat here the arguments of chapter 1—amounts to giving notice to every merchant and every manufacturer that for some time to come his stock and his raw materials will steadily depreciate on his hands, and to every one who finances his business with borrowed money that he will, sooner or later, lose 100 per cent on his liabilities

---

[1] Whilst the Conference of Genoa (April 1922) affirmed the doctrine in general, representatives of the countries chiefly affected were united in declaring that it must not be applied to them in particular. Signor Peano, M. Picard, and M. Theunis, speaking on behalf of Italy, France, and Belgium, announced, each for his own country, that they would have nothing to do with devaluating, and were determined to restore their respective currencies to their pre-war values. Reform is not likely to come by joint, simultaneous action. The experts of Genoa recognised this when they 'ventured to suggest' that 'a considerable service will be rendered by that country which first decides boldly to set the example of securing immediate stability in terms of gold' by devaluation.

(since he will have to pay back in terms of commodities twice as much as he has borrowed). Modern business, being carried on largely with borrowed money, must necessarily be brought to a standstill by such a process. It will be to the interest of everyone in business to go out of business for the time being; and of everyone who is contemplating expenditure to postpone his orders so long as he can. The wise man will be he who turns his assets into cash, withdraws from the risks and the exertions of activity, and awaits in country retirement, the steady appreciation promised him in the value of his cash. A probable expectation of deflation is bad enough; a certain expectation is disastrous. For the mechanism of the modern business world is even less adapted to fluctuations in the value of money upwards than it is to fluctuations downwards.

In the second place, in many countries, deflation, even were it desirable, is not *possible*; that is to say, deflation in sufficient degree to restore the currency to its pre-war parity. For the burden which it would throw on the taxpayer would be insupportable. I need add nothing on this to what I have already written in the second chapter above. This practical impossibility might have rendered the policy innocuous, if it were not that, by standing in the way of the alternative policy, it prolongs the period of uncertainty and severe seasonal fluctuation, and even, in some cases, can be carried into effect sufficiently to cause much interference with business. The fact, that the restoration of their currencies to the pre-war parity is still the declared official policy of the French and Italian governments, is preventing, in those countries, any rational discussion of currency reform. All those—and in the financial world they are many—who have reasons for wishing to appear 'correct', are compelled to talk foolishly. In Italy, where sound economic views have much influence and which may be nearly ripe for currency reform, Signor Mussolini has threatened to raise the lira to its former value. Fortunately for the Italian taxpayer and Italian business, the lira does not listen even to a dictator and cannot be given castor oil. But such talk can postpone positive reform; though it may be doubted if so good a politician would have propounded such a policy, even in bravado and exuberance, if he had understood that, expressed in other but equivalent words, it was as follows: 'My policy is to halve wages, double the burden of the National Debt, and to reduce by 50 per cent the prices which Sicily can get for her exports of oranges and lemons.'

One single country—Czechoslovakia—has made the experiment on a modest but sufficient scale. Comparatively free from the burden of internal debt, and free also from serious budgetary deficits, Czechoslovakia was able in the course of 1922, in pursuance of the policy of her finance minister, Dr Alois Rasin, to employ the proceeds of certain foreign loans to improve the exchange value of the Czech crown to nearly three times the rate which had been touched in the previous year. The policy has cost her an industrial crisis and serious unemployment. To what purpose? I do not know. Even now the Czech crown is not worth a sixth of its pre-war parity: and it remains unstabilised, fluttering before the breath of the seasons and the wind of politics. Is, therefore, the process of appreciation to continue indefinitely? If not, when and at what point is stabilisation to be effected? Czechoslovakia was better placed than any country in Europe to establish her economic life on the basis of a sound and fixed currency. Her finances were in equilibrium, her credit good, her foreign resources adequate, and no one could have blamed her for devaluating the crown, ruined by no fault of hers and inherited from the Habsburg empire. Pursuing a misguided policy in a spirit of stern virtue, she preferred the stagnation of her industries and a still fluctuating standard.[1]

---

[1] I cannot criticise the work, in his second term of office (1922), of Dr Rasin, now fallen by the hand of an assassin, without reference to his great achievement during his first term (1919) in rescuing his country's currency from the surrounding chaos. The stamping of the Austrian notes and the levy on holders of titles to money which accompanied it was the only drastic, courageous, and successful measure of finance carried through anywhere in Europe at that epoch: the story of it from Dr Rasin's own pen can be read in his *The Financial Policy of Czecho-Slovakia*. Before he had finished other influences became dominant. But, when in 1922 this austere and disinterested minister returned to

If the restoration of many European currencies to their pre-war parity with gold is neither desirable nor possible, what are the forces or the arguments which have established this undesirable impossibility as the avowed policy of most of them? The following are the most important:

1. *To leave the gold value of a country's currency at the low level to which war has driven it is an injustice to the* rentier *class and to others whose income is fixed in terms of currency, and practically a breach of contract; whilst to restore its value would meet a debt of honour.*

The injury done to pre-war holders of fixed interest-bearing stocks is beyond dispute. Real justice, indeed, might require the restoration of the purchasing power, and not merely the gold value, of their money incomes, a measure which no one in fact proposes; whilst nominal justice has not been infringed, since these investments were not in gold bullion but in the legal tender of the realm. Nevertheless, if this class of investors could be dealt with separately, considerations of equity and the expedience of satisfying reasonable expectation would furnish a strong case.

But this is not the actual situation. The vast issues of war loans have swamped the pre-war holdings of fixed interest-bearing stocks, and society has largely adjusted itself to the new situation. To restore the value of pre-war holdings by deflation means enhancing at the same time the value of war and post-war holdings, and thereby raising the total claims of the *rentier* class not only beyond what they are entitled to, but to an intolerable proportion of the total income of the community. Indeed justice, rightly weighed, comes down on the other side. Much the greater proportion of the money contracts still outstanding were entered into when money was worth more nearly what it is worth now than what it was worth in 1913. Thus, in order to do justice to a minority of creditors, a great injustice would be done to a great majority of debtors.

office, he missed, in my judgment, his opportunity. He could have completed his task by establishing the currency on a fixed and stable basis, instead of which he used his great authority to disorder trade by a futile process of deflation.

This aspect of the matter has been admirably argued by Professor Irving Fisher.[1] We forget, he says, that not all contracts require the same adjustment in order to secure justice, and that while we are debating whether we ought to deflate to secure ideal justice for those who made contracts on old price levels, new contracts are constantly being made at the new price levels. An estimate of the volume of contracts now outstanding, classified according to their age, would show that some contracts are a day old, some are a month old, some are a year old, some are a decade old, and some are a century old, the great mass, however, being of very recent origin. Consequently the average, or centre of gravity, of the total existing indebtedness is probably always somewhat near the present. Before the war, Professor Fisher estimated, very roughly, that contracts in the United States were on the average about one year old.

When, therefore, the depreciation of the currency has lasted long enough for society to adjust itself to the new values, deflation is even worse than inflation. Both are 'unjust' and disappoint reasonable expectation. But whereas inflation, by easing the burden of national debt and stimulating enterprise, has a little to throw into the other side of the balance, deflation has nothing.

2. *The restoration of a currency to its pre-war gold value enhances a country's financial prestige and promotes future confidence.*

Where a country can hope to restore its pre-war parity at an early date, this argument cannot be neglected. This might be said of Great Britain, Holland, Sweden, Switzerland, and (perhaps) Spain, but of no other European country. The argument cannot be extended to those countries which, even if they could raise somewhat the value of their legal-tender money, could not possibly restore it to its old value. It is of the essence of the argument that the *exact* pre-war parity should be recovered. It would not make much difference to the financial prestige of Italy whether she stabilised the lira at 100 to the £ sterling or at 60; and it

---

[1] In his article 'Devaluation *versus* Deflation', published in the eleventh *Manchester Guardian* Reconstruction Supplement (7 December 1922).

would be much better for her prestige to stabilise it definitely at 100 than to let it fluctuate between 60 and 100.

This argument is limited, therefore, to those countries the gold value of whose currencies is within (say) 5 or 10 per cent of their former value. Its force in these cases depends, I think, upon what answer we give to the problem discussed below, namely, whether we intend to pin ourselves in the future, as in the past, to an unqualified gold standard. If we still prefer such a standard to any available alternative, and if future 'confidence' in our currency is to depend not on the stability of its purchasing power but on the fixity of its gold value, then it may be worth our while to stand the racket of deflation to the extent of 5 or 10 per cent. This view is in accordance with that expressed by Ricardo in analogous circumstances a hundred years ago.[1] If, on the other hand, we decide to aim for the future at stability of the price level rather than at a fixed parity with gold, in that case *cadit quaestio*.

In any case this argument does not affect our main conclusion, that the right policy for countries of which the currency has suffered a prolonged and severe depreciation is to *devaluate*, and to fix the value of the currency at that figure in the neighbour-hood of the existing value to which commerce and wages are adjusted.

3. *If the gold value of a country's currency can be increased, labour will profit by a reduced cost of living, foreign goods will be obtainable cheaper, and foreign debts fixed in terms of gold (e.g. to the United States) will be discharged with less effort.*

This argument, which is pure delusion, exercises quite as much influence as the other two. If the franc is worth more, wages, it is argued, which are paid in francs, will surely buy more, and French imports, which are paid for in francs, will be so much cheaper. No! If francs are worth more they will buy more labour as well as more goods—that is to say, wages will fall; and the French exports, which pay for the imports, will, measured in francs, fall in value just as much as the imports. Nor will it make

---

[1] See below, p. 125.

in the long run any difference whatever in the amount of goods the value of which England will have to transfer to America to pay her dollar debts, whether in the end sterling settles down at four dollars to the pound, or at its pre-war parity. The burden of this debt depends on the value of gold, in terms of which it is fixed, not on the value of sterling. It is not easy, it seems, for men to apprehend that their money is a mere intermediary, without significance in itself, which flows from one hand to another, is received and is dispensed, and disappears when its work is done from the sum of a nation's wealth.

In concluding this section, let me quote on the issue between deflation and devaluation two classic authorities, Gibbon and Ricardo, the one to represent the imposing but false wisdom of the would-be upright statesman, the other to speak in clear tones the voice of instructed reason.

In the eleventh chapter of *The Decline and Fall*, Gibbon deems incredible a story of how in A.D. 274 Aurelian's deflationary zeal to restore the integrity of the coin excited an insurrection which caused the death of 7,000 soldiers. 'We might naturally expect', he says, 'that the reformation of the coin should have been an action equally popular with the destruction of those obsolete accounts, which by the emperor's order were burnt in the forum of Trajan. In an age when the principles of commerce were so imperfectly understood, the most desirable end might perhaps be effected by harsh and injudicious means; but a temporary grievance of such a nature can scarcely excite and support a serious civil war. The repetition of intolerable taxes, imposed either on the land or on the necessaries of life, may at least provoke those who will not or who cannot relinquish their country. But the case is far otherwise in every operation which, by whatsoever expedients, restores the just value of money.'

Rome may have understood the principles of commerce imperfectly in the third century and not perfectly in the twentieth; but that does not save her citizens from experiencing their applications. Signor Mussolini might peruse with interest the annals of Aurelian, who, 'ignorant or impatient of the restraints of civil institutions', fell by the hand of an assassin within a year of his deflation of the currency, 'regretted by the army, detested by the Senate, but universally acknowledged as a warlike and fortunate prince, the useful though severe reformer of a degenerate State'.

Ricardo, speaking in the House of Commons on the 12th of June 1822,[1] gave his opinion that: 'If in the year 1819 the value of the currency had stood at 14*s* for the pound note, which was the case in the year 1813, he should have thought that, on a balance of all the advantages and disadvantages of the case, it would have been as well to fix the currency at the then value, according to which most of the existing contracts had been made; but when the currency was within 5 per cent of its par value, he thought they had made the best selection in recurring to the old standard.'

The same is repeated in his *Protection to Agriculture*,[2] where he approves the restoration of the old standard when gold was £4. 2*s* per standard ounce, but adds that, if it had been £5. 10*s*, 'no measure could have been more inexpedient than to make so violent a change in all subsisting engagements'.

2. *Stability of prices* versus *stability of exchange*

Since, subject to the qualification of chapter 3, the rate of exchange of a country's currency with the currency of the rest of the world (assuming for the sake of simplicity that there is only one external currency) depends on the relation between the internal price level and the external price level, it follows that the exchange cannot be stable unless *both* internal *and* external price levels remain stable. If, therefore, the external price level lies

[1] The great debate of 11 and 12 June 1822, on Mr Western's motion concerning the resumption of cash payments, well illustrates, more particularly in the speeches of the opener, Mr Western, and of the opposer, Mr Huskisson, the regularity of the evils which follow a deflationary raising of the standard, and the unchanging antithesis between the temperaments of deflationists and devaluers, though I doubt if any present-day deflationists could make a speech at the same time so able and so unfair as Mr Huskisson's.

[2] *Works*, p. 468.

outside our control, we must submit either to our own internal price level or to our exchange being pulled about by external influences. If the external price level is unstable, we cannot keep *both* our own price level *and* our exchanges stable. And we are compelled to choose.

In pre-war days, when almost the whole world was on a gold standard, we had all plumped for stability of exchange as against stability of prices, and we were ready to submit to the social consequences of a change of price level for causes quite outside our control, connected, for example, with the discovery of new gold mines in foreign countries or a change of banking policy abroad. But we submitted, partly because we did not dare trust ourselves to a less automatic (though more reasoned) policy, and partly because the price fluctuations experienced were in fact moderate. Nevertheless, there were powerful advocates of the other choice. In particular, the proposals of Professor Irving Fisher for a compensated dollar amounted, unless all countries adopted the same plan, to putting into practice a preference for stability of internal price level over stability of external exchange.

The right choice is not necessarily the same for all countries. It must partly depend on the relative importance of foreign trade in the economic life of the country. Nevertheless, there does seem to be in almost every case a presumption in favour of the stability of prices, if only it can be achieved. Stability of exchange is in the nature of a convenience which adds to the efficiency and prosperity of those who are engaged in foreign trade. Stability of prices, on the other hand, is profoundly important for the avoidance of the various evils described in chapter 1. Contracts and business expectations, which presume a stable exchange, must be far fewer, even in a trading country such as England, than those which presume a stable level of internal prices. The main argument to the contrary seems to be that exchange stability is an easier aim to attain, since it only requires that the same standard of value should be adopted at home and abroad; whereas an internal standard, so regulated as to maintain stability in an index number of prices, is a difficult scientific innovation, never yet put into practice.

There has been an interesting example recently of a country which, more perhaps by chance than by design, has secured the advantages of a relatively stable level of internal prices at the expense of a fluctuating exchange, namely India. Public attention is so much fixed on the exchange as the test of the success of a financial policy, that the Government of India, under severe reproaches for what has happened, have not defended themselves as effectively as they might. During the boom of 1919–20, when world prices were soaring, the exchange value of the rupee was allowed to rise by successive stages, with the result that the highest level reached by the Indian index number in 1920 exceeded by only 12 per cent the average figure for 1919, whereas for England the figure was 29 per cent. The Report of the Indian Currency Committee, on which the Government of India acted somewhat clumsily without enough allowance for rapidly changing conditions, was avowedly influenced by the importance in such a country as India, especially in the political circumstances of that time, of avoiding a violent upward movement of internal prices. The most just criticism of the Government of India's action, in the light of after-events, is that they went too far in attempting to raise the rupee so high as 2s 8d—a rate not contemplated by the Currency Committee. Prices outside India never rose so high as to justify an exchange exceeding 2s 3d on the criterion of keeping Indian prices stable at the 1919 level. On the other hand, when world prices collapsed, the rupee exchange was allowed to fall with them, again with the result that the lowest point touched by the Indian index number in 1921 was only 16 per cent below the highest in 1920, whereas for England the figure was 50 per cent. The following table gives the details:

If the Government of India had been successful in stabilising the rupee–sterling exchange, they would necessarily have subjected India to a disastrous price fluctuation comparable to that

	Indian prices	English prices[1]	Value of rupee in sterling	
			Purchasing power parity	Actual exchange
Average 1919	100	100	100	100
Highest 1920	112	129	115	152
Lowest 1921	95	65	69	72
Average 1922	90	64	71	74

[1] *Statist.*

in England. Thus the unthinking assumption, in favour of the restoration of a fixed exchange as the one thing to aim at, requires more examination than it sometimes receives.

Especially is this the case if the prospect that a majority of countries will adopt the same standard is still remote. When by adopting the gold standard we could achieve stability of exchange with almost the whole world, whilst any other standard would have appeared as a solitary eccentricity, the solid advantages of certainty and convenience supported the conservative preference for gold. Nevertheless, even so, the convenience of traders and the primitive passion for solid metal might not, I think, have been adequate to preserve the dynasty of gold, if it had not been for another, half-accidental circumstance; namely, that for many years past gold had afforded not only a stable exchange but, on the whole, a stable price level also. In fact, the choice between stable exchanges and stable prices had not presented itself as an acute dilemma. And when, prior to the development of the South African mines, we seemed to be faced with a continuously falling price level, the fierceness of the bimetallic controversy testified to the discontent provoked as soon as the existing standard appeared seriously incompatible with the stability of prices.

Indeed, it is doubtful whether the pre-war system for regulating the international flow of gold would have been capable of dealing with such large or sudden divergencies between the price levels of different countries as have occurred lately. The fault of the pre-war régime, under which the rates of exchange between a country and the outside world were fixed, and the internal price level had to adjust itself thereto (i.e. was chiefly governed by external influences), was that it was too slow and insensitive in its mode of operation. The fault of the post-war régime, under which the price level mainly depends on internal influences (i.e. internal currency and credit policy) and the rates of exchange with the outside world have to adjust themselves thereto, is that it is too rapid in its effect and over-sensitive, with the result that it may act violently for merely transitory causes. Nevertheless, when the fluctuations are large and sudden, a quick reaction is necessary for the maintenance of equilibrium; and the necessity for quick reaction has been one of the factors which have rendered the pre-war method inapplicable to post-war conditions, and have made every one nervous of proclaiming a final fixation of the exchange.

We are familiar with the causal chain along which the pre-war method reached its result. If gold flowed out of the country's central reserves, this modified discount policy and the creation of credit, thus affecting the demand for, and hence the price of, the class of goods most sensitive to the ease of credit, and gradually, through the price of these goods, spreading its influence to the prices of goods generally, including those which enter into international trade, until at the new level of price foreign goods began to look dear at home and domestic goods cheap abroad, and the adverse balance was redressed. But this process might take months to work itself out. Nowadays, the gold reserves might be dangerously depleted before the compensating forces had time to operate. Moreover, the movement of the rate of interest up or down sometimes had more effect in attracting foreign capital or encouraging investment abroad than in influencing home prices. Where the disequilibrium was purely seasonal, this was an unqualified advantage; for it was much better that foreign funds should ebb and flow between the slack and the busy seasons than that prices should go up and down. But where it was due to more permanent causes, the adjustment even before the war might be imperfect; for the stimulus to foreign loans, whilst restoring the balance for the time being, might obscure the real seriousness of the situation, and enable a country to live beyond its resources for a considerable time at the risk of ultimate default.

Compare with this the instantaneous effects of the post-war method. If at the existing rate of exchange the amount of sterling offered in the exchange market during the course of the morning exceeds the amount of dollars offered, there is no gold available for export at a fixed price to bridge the gulf. Consequently the dollar rate of exchange must move until at the new rate the offerings of each of the two currencies in exchange for one another exactly balance in amount. But it is the inevitable result of this that within half an hour the relative prices of commodities entering into English–American trade, such as cotton and electrolytic copper, have adjusted themselves accordingly. Unless the American prices move to meet them half-way, the English prices immediately rise correspondent to the movement of the exchange.

This means that relative prices can be knocked about by the most fleeting influences of politics and of sentiment, and by the periodic pressure of seasonal trades. But it also means that the post-war method is a most rapid and powerful corrective of real disequilibria in the balance of international payments arising from whatever causes, and a wonderful preventive in the way of countries which are inclined to spend abroad beyond their resources.

Thus when there are violent shocks to the pre-existing equilibrium between the internal and external price levels, the pre-war method is likely to break down in practice, simply because it cannot bring about the readjustment of internal prices *quick enough*. Theoretically, of course, the pre-war method must be able to make itself effective sooner or later, provided the movement of gold is allowed to continue without restriction, until the inflation or deflation of prices has taken place to the necessary extent. But in practice there is usually a limit to the rate and to the amount by which the actual currency or the metallic backing for it can be allowed to flow abroad. If the supply of money or credit is reduced faster than social and business arrangements allow prices to fall, intolerable inconveniences result. Perhaps some of the incidents of debasement of the coinage which are sprinkled through the currency history of the late Middle Ages were really due to a similar cause. Prior to the discovery of the New World the precious metals were, over a long period, becoming progressively scarcer in Europe through natural wastage in the absence of adequate new supplies, and the drain to the East; with the result that from time to time the price level in England (for example) would be established on too high a level in relation to European prices. The resulting tendency of silver to flow abroad, being accentuated perhaps by some special temporary cause, would give rise to complaints of a 'scarcity of currency', which really means an outflow of money faster than social organisation permits prices to fall. No doubt some of the debasements were helped by the fact that they profited incidentally a necessitous Exchequer. But they may have been, nevertheless, the best available expedient for meeting the currency problem.[1] We shall look on Edward III's debasements of sterling money with a more tolerant eye if we regard them as a method of carrying into effect a preference for stability of internal prices over stability of external exchanges, celebrating that monarch as an enlightened forerunner of Professor Irving Fisher in advocacy of the 'compensated dollar', only more happy than the latter in his opportunities to carry theory into practice.

The reader should notice, further, the different parts played by discount policy under the one régime and under the other. With the pre-war method discount policy is a vital part of the process for restoring equilibrium between internal and external prices. With the post-war method it is not equally indispensable, since the fluctuation of the exchanges can bring about equilibrium without its aid—though it remains, of course, as an instrument

[1] Cf. Hawtrey, *Currency and Credit*, chapter XVII.

for influencing the internal price level and through this the exchanges, if we desire to establish either the one or the other at a different level from that which would have prevailed otherwise.

3. *The restoration of a gold standard*

Our conclusions up to this point are, therefore, that, when stability of the internal price level and stability of the external exchanges are incompatible, the former is generally preferable; and that on occasions when the dilemma is acute, the preservation of the former at the expense of the latter is, fortunately perhaps, the line of least resistance.

The restoration of the gold standard (whether at the pre-war parity or at some other rate) certainly will not give us complete stability of internal prices and can only give us complete stability of the external exchanges if all other countries also restore the gold standard. The advisability of restoring it depends, therefore, on whether, on the whole, it will give us the best working compromise obtainable between the two ideals.

The advocates of gold, as against a more scientific standard, base their cause on the double contention, that in practice gold has provided and will provide a reasonably stable standard of value, and that in practice, since governing authorities lack wisdom as often as not, a managed currency will, sooner or later, come to grief. Conservatism and scepticism join arms—as they often do. Perhaps superstition comes in too; for gold still enjoys the prestige of its smell and colour.

The considerable success with which gold maintained its stability of value in the changing world of the nineteenth century was certainly remarkable. I have applauded it in the first chapter. After the discoveries of Australia and California it began to depreciate dangerously, and before the exploitation of South Africa it began to appreciate dangerously. Yet in each case it righted itself and retained its reputation.

But the conditions of the future are not those of the past. We have no sufficient ground for expecting the continuance of the special conditions which preserved a sort of balance before the war. For what are the underlying explanations of the good behaviour of gold during the nineteenth century?

In the first place, it happened that progress in the discovery of gold mines roughly kept pace with progress in other directions— a correspondence which was not altogether a matter of chance, because the progress of that period, since it was characterised by the gradual opening up and exploitation of the world's surface, not unnaturally brought to light *pari passu* the remoter deposits of gold. But this stage of history is now almost at an end. A quarter of a century has passed by since the discovery of an important deposit. Material progress is more dependent now on the growth of scientific and technical knowledge, of which the application to gold-mining may be intermittent. Years may elapse without great improvement in the methods of extracting gold; and then the genius of a chemist may realise past dreams and forgotten hoaxes, transmuting base into precious like Subtle, or extracting gold from sea-water as in the Bubble. Gold is liable to be either too dear or too cheap. In either case, it is too much to expect that a succession of accidents will keep the metal steady.

But there was another type of influence which used to aid stability. The value of gold has not depended on the policy or the decisions of a single body of men; and a sufficient proportion of the supply has been able to find its way, without any flooding of the market, into the arts or into the hoards of Asia for its marginal value to be governed by a steady psychological estimation of the metal in relation to other things. This is what is meant by saying that gold has 'intrinsic value' and is free from the dangers of a 'managed' currency. The *independent variety* of the influences determining the value of gold has been in itself a steadying influence. The arbitrary and variable character of the proportion of gold reserves to liabilities maintained by many of the note-issuing banks of the world, so far from introducing an incalculable factor, was an element of stability. For when gold was relatively abundant and flowed towards them, it was absorbed by their allowing their ratio of gold reserves to rise slightly; and when it was relatively scarce, the fact that they had no intention of ever utilising their gold reserves for any practical purpose, permitted most of them to view with equanimity a moderate weakening of their proportion. A great part of the flow of South African gold between the end of the Boer War and 1914 was able to find its way into the central gold reserves of European and other countries with the minimum effect on prices.

But the war has effected a great change. Gold itself has become a 'managed' currency. The West, as well as the East, has learnt to hoard gold; but the motives of the United States are not those of India. Now that most countries have abandoned the gold standard, the supply of the metal would, if the chief user of it restricted its holdings to its real needs, prove largely redundant. The United States has not been able to let gold fall to its 'natural' value, because it could not face the resulting depreciation of its standard. It has been driven, therefore, to the costly policy of burying in the vaults of Washington what the miners of the Rand have laboriously brought to the surface. Consequently gold now stands at an 'artificial' value, the future course of which almost entirely depends on the policy of the Federal Reserve Board of the United States. The value of gold is no longer the resultant of the chance gifts of Nature and the judgment of numerous authorities and individuals acting independently. Even if other countries gradually return to a gold basis, the position will not be greatly changed. The tendency to employ some variant of the gold-exchange standard and the probably permanent disappearance of gold from the pockets of the people are likely to mean that the strictly *necessary* gold reserves of the central banks of the gold-standard countries will fall considerably short of the available supplies. The actual value of gold will depend, therefore, on the policy of three or four of the most powerful central banks, whether they act independently or in unison. If, on the other hand, pre-war conventions about the use of gold in reserves and in circulation were to be restored—which is, in my opinion, the much less probable alternative—there might be, as Professor Cassel has predicted, a serious shortage of gold leading to a progressive appreciation in its value.

Nor must we neglect the possibility of a partial demonetisation of gold by the United States through a closing of its mints to further receipts of gold. The present policy of the United States in accepting unlimited imports of gold can be justified, perhaps, as a temporary measure, intended to preserve tradition and to strengthen confidence through a transitional period. But, looked at as a permanent arrangement, it could hardly be judged otherwise than as a foolish expense. If the Federal Reserve Board intends to maintain the value of the dollar at a level which is irrespective of the inflow or outflow of gold, what object is there in continuing to accept at the mints gold which is not wanted, yet costs a heavy price? If the United States mints were to be closed to gold, everything, except the actual price of the metal, could continue precisely as before.

Confidence in the future stability of the value of gold depends therefore on the United States being foolish enough to go on accepting gold which it does not want, and wise enough, having accepted it, to maintain it at a fixed value. This double event might be realised through the collaboration of a public under-standing nothing with a Federal Reserve Board understanding everything. But the position is precarious; and not very attractive to any country which is still in a position to choose what its future standard is to be.

This discussion of the prospects of the stability of gold has partly answered by anticipation the second principal argument in favour of the restoration of an unqualified gold standard, namely that this is the only way of avoiding the dangers of a 'managed' currency.

It is natural, after what we have experienced, that prudent people should desiderate a standard of value which is independent of finance ministers and state banks. The present state of affairs has allowed to the ignorance and frivolity of statesmen an ample opportunity of bringing about ruinous consequences in the economic field. It is felt that the general level of economic and financial education amongst statesmen and bankers is hardly such as to render innovations feasible or safe; that, in fact, a chief object of stabilising the exchanges is to strap down ministers of finance.

These are reasonable grounds of hesitation. But the experience on which they are based is by no means fair to the capacities of statesmen and bankers. The non-metallic standards, of which we have experience, have been anything rather than scientific experiments coolly carried out. They have been a last resort, involuntarily adopted, as a result of war or inflationary taxation, when the state finances were already broken or the situation out of hand. Naturally in these circumstances such practices have been the accompaniment and the prelude of disaster. But we cannot argue from this to what can be achieved in normal times. I do not see that the regulation of the standard of value is essentially more difficult than many other objects of less social necessity which we attain successfully.

If, indeed, a providence watched over gold, or if Nature had provided us with a stable standard ready-made, I would not, in an attempt after some slight improvement, hand over the management to the possible weakness or ignorance of boards and governments. But this is not the situation. We have no ready-made standard. Experience has shown that in emergencies ministers of finance cannot be strapped down. And—most important of all— in the modern world of paper currency and bank credit there is no escape from a 'managed' currency, whether we wish it or not; convertibility into gold will not alter the fact that the value of gold itself depends on the policy of the central banks.

It is worth while to pause a moment over the last sentence. It differs significantly from the doctrine of gold reserves which we learnt and taught before the war. We used to assume that no central bank would be so extravagant as to keep more gold than it required or so imprudent as to keep less. From time to time gold would flow out into the circulation or for export abroad; experience showed that the quantity required on these occasions bore some rough proportion to the central bank's liabilities; a decidedly higher proportion than this would be fixed on to provide for contingencies and to inspire confidence; and the creation of credit would be regulated largely by reference to the maintenance of this proportion. The Bank of England, for example, would allow itself to be swayed by the tides of gold, permitting the inflowing and outflowing streams to produce their 'natural' consequences unchecked by any ideas as to preventing the effect on prices. Already before the war, the system was becoming precarious by reason of its artificiality. The 'proportion' was by the lapse of time losing its relation to the facts and had become largely conventional. Some other figure, greater or less, would have done just as well.[1] The war broke down the convention; for the withdrawal of gold from actual circulation destroyed one of the elements of reality lying behind the convention, and the suspension of convertibility destroyed the other. It would have been absurd to regulate the bank rate by reference to a 'proportion' which had lost all its significance; and in the course of the past ten years a new policy has been evolved. The bank rate is now employed, however incompletely and experimentally, to regulate the expansion and deflation of credit in the interests of business stability and the steadiness of prices. In so far as it is employed to procure stability of the dollar exchange, where this is inconsistent with stability of internal prices, we have a relic of pre-war policy and a compromise between discrepant aims.

Those who advocate the return to a gold standard do not always appreciate along what different lines our actual practice has been drifting. If we restore the gold standard, are we to return also to the pre-war conceptions of bank rate, allowing the tides of gold to play what tricks they like with the internal price level, and abandoning the attempt to moderate the disastrous influence of the credit cycle on the stability of prices and

---

[1] See, for what I wrote about this in 1914, *The Economic Journal*, XXIV, p. 621.

employment? Or are we to continue and develop the experimental innovations of our present policy, ignoring the 'bank ratio' and, if necessary, allowing unmoved a piling up of gold reserves far beyond our requirements or their depletion far below them?

In truth, the gold standard is already a barbarous relic. All of us, from the Governor of the Bank of England downwards, are now primarily interested in preserving the stability of business, prices, and employment, and are not likely, when the choice is forced on us, deliberately to sacrifice these to the outworn dogma, which had its value once, of £3. 17s 10½d per ounce. Advocates of the ancient standard do not observe how remote it now is from the spirit and the requirements of the age. A regulated non-metallic standard has slipped in unnoticed. *It exists*. Whilst the economists dozed, the academic dream of a hundred years, doffing its cap and gown, clad in paper rags, has crept into the real world by means of the bad fairies—always so much more potent than the good—the wicked ministers of finance.

For these reasons enlightened advocates of the restoration of gold, such as Mr Hawtrey, do not welcome it as the return of a 'natural' currency, and intend, quite decidedly, that it shall be a 'managed' one. They allow gold back only as a constitutional monarch, shorn of his ancient despotic powers and compelled to accept the advice of a Parliament of banks. The adoption of the ideas present in the minds of those who drafted the Genoa Resolutions on Currency is an essential condition of Mr Hawtrey's adherence to gold. He contemplates 'the practice of continuous co-operation among central banks of issue' (Resolution 3), and an international convention, based on a gold-exchange standard, and designed 'with a view to preventing undue fluctuations in the purchasing power of gold' (Resolution 11).[1] But he is *not* in favour of resuming the gold standard irrespective of 'whether the difficulties in regard to the future purchasing power of gold have been provided against or not'. 'It is not easy', he

---

[1] *Monetary Reconstruction*, p. 132.

admits, 'to promote international action, and should it fail, the wisest course for the time being might be to concentrate on the stabilisation of sterling in terms of commodities, rather than tie the pound to a metal, the vagaries of which cannot be foreseen.'[1]

It is natural to ask, in face of advocacy of this kind, why it is necessary to drag in gold at all. Mr Hawtrey lays no stress on the obvious support for his compromise, namely the force of sentiment and tradition, and the preference of Englishmen for shearing a monarch of his powers rather than of his head. But he adduces three other reasons: (1) that gold is required as a liquid reserve for the settlement of international balances of indebtedness; (2) that it enables an experiment to be made without cutting adrift from the old system; and (3) that the vested interests of gold producers must be considered. These objects, however, are so largely attained by my own suggestions in the following chapter, that I need not dwell on them here.

On the other hand, I see grave objections to reinstating gold in the pious hope that international co-operation will keep it in order. With the existing distribution of the world's gold, the reinstatement of the gold standard means, inevitably, that we surrender the regulation of our price level and the handling of the credit cycle to the Federal Reserve Board of the United States. Even if the most intimate and cordial co-operation is established between the Board and the Bank of England, the preponderance of power will still belong to the former. The Board will be in a position to disregard the Bank. But if the Bank disregard the Board, it will render itself liable to be flooded with, or depleted of, gold, as the case may be. Moreover, we can be confident beforehand that there will be much suspicion amongst Americans (for that is their disposition) of any supposed attempt on the part of the Bank of England to dictate their policy or to influence American discount rates in the interests of Great Britain. We must also be prepared to incur our share of the vain expense of bottling up the world's redundant gold.

[1] *Loc. cit.* p. 22.

It would be rash in present circumstances to surrender our freedom of action to the Federal Reserve Board of the United States. We do not yet possess sufficient experience of its capacity to act in times of stress with courage and independence. The Federal Reserve Board is striving to free itself from the pressure of sectional interests; but we are not yet certain that it will wholly succeed. It is still liable to be overwhelmed by the impetuosity of a cheap money campaign. A suspicion of British influence would, so far from strengthening the Board, greatly weaken its resistance to popular clamour. Nor is it certain, quite apart from weakness or mistakes, that the simultaneous application of the same policy will always be in the interests of both countries. The development of the credit cycle and the state of business may sometimes be widely different on the two sides of the Atlantic.

Therefore, since I regard the stability of prices, credit, and employment as of paramount importance, and since I feel no confidence that an old-fashioned gold standard will even give us the modicum of stability that it used to give, I reject the policy of restoring the gold standard on pre-war lines. At the same time I doubt the wisdom of attempting a 'managed' gold standard jointly with the United States, on the lines recommended by Mr Hawtrey, because it retains too many of the disadvantages of the old system without its advantages, and because it would make us too dependent on the policy and on the wishes of the Federal Reserve Board.

Chapter 5

POSITIVE SUGGESTIONS
FOR THE FUTURE REGULATION
OF MONEY

A sound constructive scheme must provide—if it is to satisfy the arguments and the analysis of this book:

1. A method for regulating the supply of currency and credit with a view to maintaining, so far as possible, the stability of the internal price level; and

2. A method for regulating the supply of foreign exchange so as to avoid purely temporary fluctuations, caused by seasonal or other influences and not due to a lasting disturbance in the relation between the internal and the external price level.

I believe that in Great Britain the ideal system can be most nearly and most easily reached by an adaptation of the actual system which has grown up, half haphazard, since the war. After the general idea has been exhibited by an application in detail to the case of Great Britain, it will be sufficient to deal somewhat briefly with the modifications required in the case of other countries.

1. *Great Britain*

The system actually in operation to-day is broadly as follows:

(1) The internal price level is mainly determined by the amount of credit created by the banks, chiefly the Big Five; though in a depression, when the public are increasing their real balances, a greater amount of credit has to be created to support a given price level (in accordance with the theory explained above in chapter 3, p. 61) than is required in a boom, when real balances are being diminished.

The amount of credit, so created, is in its turn roughly

measured by the volume of the banks' deposits—since variations in this total must correspond to variations in the total of their investments, bill-holdings, and advances. Now there is no necessary reason *a priori* why the proportion between the banks' deposits and their 'cash in hand and at the Bank of England' should not fluctuate within fairly wide limits in accordance with circumstances. But in practice the banks usually work by rule of thumb and do not depart widely from their preconceived 'proportions'.[1] In recent times their aggregate deposits have always been about nine times their 'cash'. Since this is what is generally considered a 'safe' proportion, it is bad for a bank's reputation to fall below it, whilst on the other hand it is bad for its earning power to rise above it. Thus in one way or another the banks generally adjust their total creation of credit in one form or another (investments, bills, and advances) up to their capacity as measured by the above criterion; from which it follows that the volume of their 'cash' in the shape of bank and currency notes and deposits at the Bank of England closely determines the volume of credit which they create.

In order to follow, therefore, the train of causation a stage further, we must consider what determines the volume of their 'cash'. Its amount can only be altered in one or other of three ways: (*a*) by the public requiring more or fewer notes in circulation, (*b*) by the Treasury borrowing more or less from the Currency Note Account, and (*c*) by the Bank of England increasing or diminishing its assets.[2]

To complete the argument, one further factor, not yet mentioned, must be introduced, namely (*d*) the proportion of the

---

[1] The joint stock banks have published monthly returns since January 1921. Excluding the half-yearly statement when a little 'window-dressing' is temporarily arranged, the extreme range of fluctuation has been between 11·0 per cent and 11·9 per cent in the proportion of 'cash' to deposits, and between 41·1 per cent and 50·1 per cent in the proportion of advances to deposits. These figures cover two and a half years of widely varying conditions. The 'proportions' of individual banks differ amongst themselves, and the above is an average result, the steadiness of which is strengthened by the fact that each big bank is pretty steadfast in its own policy.

[2] For the aggregate of its liabilities in the shape of deposits and of notes in circulation automatically depends on the volume of its assets.

banks' second-line reserve in the shape of their holdings of Treasury bills, which can be regarded as cash at one remove. In determining what is a safe proportion of 'cash', they pay some regard to the amount of Treasury bills which they hold, since by reducing this holding they can immediately increase their 'cash' and compel the Treasury to borrow more either from the Currency Note Account or from the Bank of England. The nine-fold proportion referred to above presumes a certain minimum holding of Treasury bills, and might have to be modified if a sufficient volume of such bills was not available. This factor (d) is, however, also important because the banks in their turn are open to pressure by the Treasury, whenever it draws to itself the resources of their depositors—whether by taxation or by offering them attractive longer-dated loans—and uses them to pay off, if not Ways and Means advances from the Bank of England (which reduces the banks' first-line reserve of cash), then alternatively Treasury bills held by the banks themselves (which reduces their second-line reserve of bills).

Items (a), (b), (c), and (d) together, therefore, more or less settle the matter. For the purpose of the present argument, however, we need not pay much separate attention to (a) and (b), since their effect is, for the most part, reflected over again in (c) and (d). (a) depends partly on the volume of trade but mainly on the price level itself; and in practice fluctuations in (a) do not *directly* affect the banks' 'cash', for if more notes are required under (a), more notes are issued, the Treasury borrowing a corresponding additional amount from the Currency Note Account, in which case the Treasury either repays the Bank of England, which diminishes the Bank's assets and consequently the other banks' 'cash', or withdraws an equivalent amount of Treasury bills, which diminishes the other banks' second-line reserve; i.e. a change in (a) operates on the banks' resources through (c) and (d).[1] Whilst as for (b), a change in the amount of

---

[1] If the additional issue of notes is covered by transferring gold from the Bank of England, this is merely an alternative way of diminishing the Bank of England's assets.

what the Treasury borrows from the Currency Note Account is reflected by a corresponding change in the opposite sense in what it borrows in Ways and Means advances or in Treasury bills.

Thus we can concentrate our attention on (*c*) and (*d*) as the main determining factors of the price level.

Now (*c*), namely the assets of the Bank of England, consist (so far as their variable part is concerned) of (i) Ways and Means advances to the Treasury, (ii) gilt-edged and other investments, (iii) advances to its customers and bills of exchange, (iv) gold. An increase in any of these items tends, therefore, to increase the other banks' 'cash', thereby to stimulate the creation of credit, and hence to raise the price level; and contrariwise.

And (*d*), namely the banks' holdings of Treasury bills, depend on the excess of the expenditure of the Treasury over and above what it secures (i) from the public by taxation and loans, (ii) from the Bank of England in Ways and Means advances, and (iii) by borrowing from the Currency Note Account.

It follows that the capacity of the joint stock banks to create credit is mainly governed by the policies and actions of the Bank of England and of the Treasury. When these are settled, (*a*), (*b*), (*c*), and (*d*) are settled.

How far can these two authorities control their own actions and how far must they remain passive agents? In my opinion the control, if they choose to exercise it, is mainly in their own hands. As regards the Treasury, the extent to which they draw money from the public to discharge floating debt clearly depends on the rate of interest and the type of loan which they are prepared to offer. A point might be reached when they could not fund further on any reasonable terms; but within fairly wide limits the policy of the Treasury can be whatever the Chancellor of the Exchequer and the House of Commons may decide. The Bank of England also is, within sufficiently wide limits, mistress of the situation if she acts in conjunction with the Treasury. She can increase or decrease at will her investments and her gold by buying or selling the one or the other. In the case of advances and of bills, whilst their volume is not so immediately or directly controllable, here also adequate control can be obtained by varying the price charged, that is to say the bank rate.[1]

Therefore it is broadly true to say that the level of prices, and hence the level of the exchanges, depends in the last resort on the policy of the Bank of England and of the Treasury in respect of the above particulars; though the other banks, if they strongly opposed the official policy, could thwart, or at least delay it to a certain extent—provided they were prepared to depart from their usual proportions.

(2) Cash, in the form of bank or currency notes, is supplied *ad libitum*, i.e. in such quantities as are called for by the amount of credit created and the internal price level established under (1). That is to say, in practice; in theory, a limit to the issue of currency notes has been laid down, namely the maximum fiduciary issue actually attained in the preceding calendar year. Since this theoretical maximum was prescribed, it has never yet been actually operative; and, as the rule springs from a doctrine now out of date and out of accordance with most responsible opinion, it is probable that, if it were becoming operative, it would be relaxed. This is a matter where the recommendations of the Cunliffe Committee call for urgent change, unless we desire deliberately to pursue still further a process of deflation. A point must come when, a year of brisk trade and employment following one of depression, there will be an increased demand for currency,

---

[1] It is often assumed that the bank rate is the *sole* governing factor. But the bank rate can only operate by its reaction on (c), namely, the Bank of England's assets. Formerly it acted pretty directly on two of the components of (c), namely, (c)(iii) advances to customers and bills of exchange and (c)(iv) gold. Now it acts only on one of them, namely, (c)(iii). But changes in (c) (i) the Bank's advances to the Treasury and (c) (ii) the Bank's investments can often be nearly as potent in their effect on the creation of credit. Thus a low bank rate can be largely neutralised by a simultaneous reduction of (c)(i) or (c)(ii) and a high bank rate by an increase of these. Indeed the Bank of England can probably bring the money market to heel more decisively by buying or selling securities than in any other way; and the utility of bank rate, operated by itself and without assistance from deliberate variations in the volume of (c)(ii), is lessened by the various limitations which exist in practice to its freedom of movement, and to the limits within which it can move, upwards and downwards.

which must be met unless the revival is to be deliberately damped down.

Thus the tendency of today—rightly I think—is to watch and to control the creation of credit and to let the creation of currency follow suit, rather than, as formerly, to watch and to control the creation of currency and to let the creation of credit follow suit.

(3) The Bank of England's gold is immobilised. It neither buys nor sells. The gold plays no part in our system. Occasionally, however, the Bank may ship a consignment to the United States, to help the Treasury in meeting its dollar liabilities. The South African and other gold which finds its way here comes purely as a commodity to a convenient *entrepôt* centre, and is mostly re-exported.

(4) The foreign exchanges are unregulated and left to look after themselves. From day to day they fluctuate in accordance with the seasons and other irregular influences. Over longer periods they depend, as we have seen, on the relative price levels established here and abroad by the respective credit policies adopted here and abroad. But whilst this is, for the most part, the actual state of affairs, it is not, as yet, the avowed or consistent policy of the responsible authorities. Fixity of the dollar exchange at the pre-war parity remains their aspiration; and it still may happen that the bank rate is raised for the purpose of influencing the exchange at a time when considerations of internal price level and credit policy point the other way.

This, in brief—I apologise to the reader if I have compressed the argument unduly—is the present state of affairs, one essentially different from our pre-war system. It will be observed that in practice we have already gone a long way towards the ideal of directing bank rate and credit policy by reference to the internal price level and other symptoms of under- or over-expansion of internal credit, rather than by reference to the pre-war criteria of the amount of cash in circulation (or of gold reserves in the banks) or the level of the dollar exchange.

1. Accordingly my first requirement in a good constructive scheme can be supplied merely by a development of our existing arrangements on more deliberate and self-conscious lines. Hitherto the Treasury and the Bank of England have looked forward to the stability of the dollar exchange (preferably at the pre-war parity) as their objective. It is not clear whether they intend to stick to this irrespective of fluctuations in the value of the dollar (or of gold); whether, that is to say, they would sacrifice the stability of sterling prices to the stability of the dollar exchange in the event of the two proving to be incompatible. At any rate, my scheme would require that they should adopt the stability of sterling prices as their *primary* objective—though this would not prevent their aiming at exchange stability also as a secondary objective by co-operating with the Federal Reserve Board in a common policy. So long as the Federal Reserve Board was successful in keeping dollar prices steady the objective of keeping sterling prices steady would be identical with the objective of keeping the dollar–sterling exchange steady. My recommendation does not involve more than a determination that, in the event of the Federal Reserve Board failing to keep dollar prices steady, sterling prices should not, if it could be helped, plunge with them merely for the sake of maintaining a fixed parity of exchange.

If the Bank of England, the Treasury, and the Big Five were to adopt this policy, to what criteria should they look respectively in regulating bank rate, government borrowing, and trade advances? The first question is whether the criterion should be a precise, arithmetical formula or whether it should be sought in a general judgment of the situation based on all the available data. The pioneer of price stability as against exchange stability, Professor Irving Fisher, advocated the former in the shape of his 'compensated dollar', which was to be automatically adjusted by reference to an index number of prices without any play of judgment or discretion. He may have been influenced, however, by the advantage of propounding a method which could be grafted as easily as possible on to the pre-war system of gold reserves and gold ratios. In any case, I doubt the wisdom and the practicability of a system so cut and dried. If we wait until a price movement is actually afoot before applying remedial measures, we may be too late. 'It is not the *past* rise in prices but the *future* rise that has to be counteracted.'[1] It is characteristic of the impetuosity of the credit cycle that price movements tend to be cumulative, each movement promoting, up to a certain point, a further movement in the same direction. Professor Fisher's method may be adapted to deal with long-period trends in the value of gold but not with the, often more injurious, short-period oscillations of the credit cycle. Nevertheless, whilst it would not be advisable to postpone action until it was called for by an actual movement of prices, it would promote confidence and furnish an objective standard of value, if, an official index number having been compiled of such a character as to register the price of a standard composite commodity, the authorities were to adopt this composite commodity as their standard of value in the sense that they would employ all their resources to prevent a movement of its price by more than a certain percentage in either direction away from the normal, just as before the war they employed all their resources to prevent a movement in the price of gold by more than a certain percentage. The precise composition of the standard composite commodity could be modified from time to time in accordance with changes in the relative economic importance of its various components.

As regards the criteria, other than the actual trend of prices, which should determine the action of the controlling authority, it is beyond the scope of this volume to deal adequately with the diagnosis and analysis of the credit cycle. The more deeply that our researches penetrate into this subject, the more accurately shall we understand the right time and method for controlling credit expansion by bank rate or otherwise. But in the meantime we have a considerable and growing body of general experience

[1] Hawtrey, *Monetary Reconstruction*, p. 105.

upon which those in authority can base their judgments. Actual price movements must of course provide the most important datum; but the state of employment, the volume of production, the effective demand for credit as felt by the banks, the rate of interest on investments of various types, the volume of new issues, the flow of cash into circulation, the statistics of foreign trade and the level of the exchanges must all be taken into account. The main point is that the *objective* of the authorities, pursued with such means as are at their command, should be the stability of prices.

It would at least be possible to avoid, for example, such action as has been taken lately (in Great Britain) whereby the supply of 'cash' has been deflated at a time when real balances were becoming inflated—action which has materially aggravated the severity of the late depression. We might be able to moderate very greatly the amplitude of the fluctuations if it was understood that the time to deflate the supply of cash is when real balances are falling, i.e. when prices are rising out of proportion to the increase, if any, in the volume of cash, and that the time to inflate the supply of cash is when real balances are rising, and not, as seems to be our present practice, the other way round.

2. How can we best combine this primary object with a maximum stability of the exchanges? Can we get the best of both worlds—stability of prices over long periods and stability of exchanges over short periods? It is the great advantage of the gold standard that it overcomes the excessive sensitiveness of the exchanges to temporary influences, which we analysed in chapter 3. Our object must be to secure this advantage, if we can, without committing ourselves to follow big movements in the value of gold itself.

I believe that we can go a long way in this direction if the Bank of England will take over the duty of regulating the price of gold, just as it already regulates the rate of discount. 'Regulate', but not 'peg'. The Bank of England should have a buying and a selling price for gold, just as it did before the war, and this price might remain unchanged for considerable periods, just as bank rate does. But it would not be fixed or 'pegged' once and for all, any more than bank rate is fixed. The Bank's rate for gold would be announced every Thursday morning at the same time as its rate for discounting bills, with a difference between its buying and selling rates corresponding to the pre-war margin between £3. 17s 10½d per oz. and £3. 17s 9d per oz.; except that, in order to obviate too frequent changes in the rate, the difference might be wider than 1½d per oz.—say, ½ to 1 per cent. A willingness on the part of the Bank both to buy and to sell gold at rates fixed for the time being would keep the dollar–sterling exchange steady within corresponding limits, so that the exchange rate would not move with every breath of wind but only when the Bank had come to a considered judgment that a change was required for the sake of the stability of sterling prices.

If the bank rate and the gold rate in conjunction were leading to an excessive influx or an excessive efflux of gold, the Bank of England would have to decide whether the flow was due to an internal or to an external movement away from stability. To fix our ideas, let us suppose that gold is flowing outwards. If this seemed to be due to a tendency of sterling to depreciate in terms of commodities, the correct remedy would be to raise the bank rate. If, on the other hand, it was due to a tendency of gold to appreciate in terms of commodities, the correct remedy would be to raise the gold rate (i.e. the buying price for gold). If, however, the flow could be explained by seasonal, or other passing influences, then it should be allowed to continue (assuming, of course, that the Bank's gold reserves were equal to any probable calls on them) unchecked, to be redressed later on by the corresponding reaction.

Two subsidiary suggestions may be made for strengthening the Bank's control:

(1) The service of the American debt will make it necessary for the British Treasury to buy nearly $500,000 every working day. It is clear that the particular method adopted for purchasing

these huge sums will greatly affect the short-period fluctuations of the exchange. I suggest that this duty should be entrusted to the Bank of England to be carried out by them with the express object of minimising those fluctuations in the exchange which are due to the daily and seasonal ebb and flow of the ordinary trade demand. In particular the proper distribution of these purchases through the year might be so arranged as greatly to mitigate the normal seasonal fluctuation discussed in chapter 3. If the trade demand is concentrated in one half of the year the Treasury demand should be concentrated in the other half.

(2) It would effect an improvement in the technique of the system here proposed, without altering its fundamental characteristics, if the Bank of England were to quote a daily price, not only for the purchase and sale of gold for immediate delivery, but also for delivery three months forward. The difference, if any, between the cash and forward quotations might represent either a discount or a premium of the latter on the former, according as the Bank desired money rates in London to stand below or above those in New York. The existence of the forward quotation of the Bank of England would afford a firm foundation for a free market in forward exchange, and would facilitate the movement of funds between London and New York for short periods, in much the same way as before the war, whilst at the same time keeping down to a minimum the actual movement of gold bullion backwards and forwards. I need not develop this point further, because it is only an application of the argument of section 3 of chapter 3 which will be most readily intelligible to the reader, if he will refer back to the previous argument.

There remains the question of the regulation of the note issue. My proposal here may appear shocking until the reader realises that, apart from its disregarding the conventions, it does not differ in substance from the existing state of affairs. The object of fixing the amount of gold to be held against a note issue is to set up a danger signal which cannot be easily disregarded, when a curtailment of credit and purchasing power is urgently required to maintain the legal tender money at its lawful parity. But this system, whilst far better than no system at all, is primitive in its ideas and is, in fact, a survival of an earlier evolutionary stage in the development of credit and currency. For it has two great disadvantages. In so far as we fix a minimum gold reserve against the note issue, the effect is to immobilise this quantity of gold and thus to reduce the amount actually available for use as a store of value to meet temporary or sudden deficits in the country's international balance of payments. And in so far as we regard an approach towards the prescribed minimum or a departure upwards from it as a barometer warning us to curtail credit or encouraging us to expand it, we are using a criterion which most people would now agree in considering second-rate for the purpose, because it cannot give the necessary warning *soon enough*. If gold movements are actually taking place, this means that the disequilibrium has proceeded a very long way; and whilst this criterion may pull us up in time to preserve convertibility on the one hand or to prevent an excessive flood of gold on the other, it will not do so in time to avoid an injurious oscillation of prices. This method belongs indeed to a period when the preservation of convertibility was all that anyone thought about (all indeed that there was to think about so long as we were confined to an unregulated gold standard), and before the idea of utilising bank rate as a means of keeping prices and employment steady had become practical politics.

We have scarcely realised how far our thoughts have travelled during the past five years. But to re-read the famous Cunliffe Report on Currency and Foreign Exchange after the War, published in 1918, brings vividly before one's mind what a great distance we have covered since then. This document was published the same month as the Armistice. It was compiled long before the unpegging of sterling and the great break in the European exchanges in 1919, before the tremendous boom and crash of 1920–1, before the vast piling up of the world's gold in America, and without experience of the Federal Reserve policy in 1922-3 of burying this gold at Washington, withdrawing it from the exercise of its full effect on prices, and thereby, in effect, demonetising the metal. The Cunliffe Report is an unadulterated pre-war prescription—inevitably so considering that it was written after four years' interregnum of war, before peace was in sight, and without knowledge of the revolutionary and unforeseeable experiences of the past five years.

Of all the omissions from the Cunliffe Report the most noteworthy is the complete absence of any mention of the problem of the stability of the price level; and it cheerfully explains how the pre-war system, which it aims at restoring, operated to bring back equilibrium by deliberately causing a 'consequent slackening of employment'. The Cunliffe Report belongs to an extinct and an almost forgotten order of ideas. Few think on these lines now; yet the Report remains the authorised declaration of our policy, and the Bank of England and the Treasury are said still to regard it as their marching orders.

Let us return to the regulation of note issue. If we agree that gold is not to be employed in the circulation, and that it is better to employ some other criterion than the ratio of gold reserves to note issue in deciding to raise or to lower the bank rate, it follows that the only employment for gold (nevertheless important) is as a store of value to be held as a war-chest against emergencies and as a means of rapidly correcting the influence of a temporarily adverse balance of international payments and thus maintaining a day-to-day stability of the sterling–dollar exchange. It is desirable, therefore, that the whole of the reserves should be under the control of the authority responsible for this, which, under the above proposals, is the Bank of England. The volume of the paper money, on the other hand, would be consequential, as it is at present, on the state of trade and employment, bank-rate policy and the Treasury bill policy. The governors of the system would be bank-rate and Treasury bill policy, the objects of government would be stability of trade, prices, and employment, and the volume of paper money would be a consequence of the first (just—I repeat—as it is at present) and an instrument of the second, the precise arithmetical level of which could not and need not be predicted. Nor would the amount of gold, which it would be prudent to hold as a reserve against international emergencies and temporary indebtedness, bear any logical or calculable relation to the volume of paper money; for the two have no close or necessary connection with one another. Therefore I make the proposal—which may seem, but should not be, shocking—of separating entirely the gold reserve from the note issue. Once this principle is adopted, the regulations are matters of detail. The gold reserves of the country should be concentrated in the hands of the Bank of England, to be used for the purpose of avoiding short-period fluctuations in the exchange. The currency notes may, just as well as not—since the Treasury is to draw the profit from them—be issued by the Treasury, without the latter being subjected to any formal regulations (which are likely to be either inoperative or injurious) as to their volume. Except in form, this régime would not differ materially from the existing state of affairs.

The reader will observe that I retain for gold an important rôle in our system. As an ultimate safeguard and as a reserve for sudden requirements, no superior medium is yet available. But I urge that it is possible to get the benefit of the advantages of gold, without irrevocably binding our legal-tender money to follow blindly all the vagaries of gold and future unforeseeable fluctuations in its real purchasing power.

2. *The United States*

The above proposals are recommended to Great Britain and their details have been adapted to her case. But the principles underlying them remain just as true across the Atlantic. In the United States, as in Great Britain, the methods which are being actually pursued at the present time, half consciously and half unconsciously, are mainly on the lines I advocate. In practice the Federal Reserve Board often ignores the proportion of its gold

154

reserve to its liabilities and is influenced, in determining its discount policy, by the object of maintaining stability in prices, trade, and employment. Out of convention and conservatism it accepts gold. Out of prudence and understanding it buries it. Indeed the theory and investigation of the credit cycle have been taken up so much more enthusiastically and pushed so much further by the economists of the United States than by those of Great Britain, that it would be even more difficult for the Federal Reserve Board than for the Bank of England to ignore such ideas or to avoid being, half-consciously at least, influenced by them.

The theory on which the Federal Reserve Board is supposed to govern its discount policy, by reference to the influx and efflux of gold and the proportion of gold to liabilities, is as dead as mutton. It perished, and perished justly, as soon as the Federal Reserve Board began to ignore its ratio and to accept gold without allowing it to exercise its full influence,[1] merely because an expansion of credit and prices seemed at that moment undesirable. From that day gold was demonetised by almost the last country which still continued to do it lip-service, and a dollar standard was set up on the pedestal of the Golden Calf. For the past two years the United States has *pretended* to maintain a gold standard. *In fact* it has established a dollar standard; and, instead of ensuring that the value of the dollar shall conform to that of gold, it makes provision, at great expense, that the value of gold shall conform to that of the dollar. This is the way by which a rich country is able to combine new wisdom with old prejudice. It can enjoy the latest scientific improvements, devised in the economic laboratory of Harvard, whilst leaving Congress to believe that no rash departure will be permitted from the hard money consecrated by the wisdom and experience of Dungi, Darius, Constantine, Lord Liverpool, and Senator Aldrich.

[1] The influx of gold could not be prevented from having *some* inflationary effect because its receipt automatically increased the balances of the member banks. This uncontrollable element cannot be avoided so long as the United States mints are compelled to accept gold. But the gold was not allowed to exercise the multiplied influence which the pre-war system presumed.

No doubt it is worth the expense—for those that can afford it. The cost of the fiction to the United States is not more than £100 million per annum and should not average in the long run above £50 million per annum. But there is in all such fictions a certain instability. When the accumulations of gold heap up beyond a certain point the suspicions of Congressmen may be aroused. One cannot be quite certain that some Senator might not read and understand this book. Sooner or later the fiction will lose its value.

Indeed it is desirable that this should be so. The new methods will work more efficiently and more economically when they can be pursued consciously, deliberately, and openly. The economists of Harvard know more than those of Washington, and it will be well that in due course their surreptitious victory should swell into public triumph. At any rate those who are responsible for establishing the principles of British currency should not overlook the possibility that some day soon the mints of the United States may be closed to the acceptance of gold at a fixed dollar price.

Closing the mints to the compulsory acceptance of gold need not affect the existing obligation of convertibility—the liability to encash notes in gold might still remain. Theoretically this might be regarded as a blemish on the perfection of the scheme. But, for the present at least, it is unlikely that such a provision would compel the United States to deflate, which possibility is the only theoretical objection to it. On the other hand, the retention of convertibility would remain a safeguard satisfactory to old-fashioned people; and would reduce to a minimum the new and controversial legislation required to effect the change. Many people might agree to relieve the mints of the liability to accept gold which no one wants, who would be dismayed at any tampering with convertibility. Moreover, in certain quite possible circumstances, the obligation of convertibility might really prove to be a safeguard against inflation brought about by political pressure contrary to the judgment of the Federal Reserve Board;

for we have not, as yet, sufficient experience as to the independence of the Federal Reserve System against the farmers, for example, or other compact interests possessing political influence.

Meanwhile Mr Hoover and many banking authorities in England and America, who look to the dispersion through the world of a reasonable proportion of Washington's gold, by the natural operation of trade and investment, as a desirable and probable development, much misunderstand the situation. At present the United States is open to accept gold at a price in terms of goods above its natural value (above the value it would have, that is to say, if it were allowed to affect credit and, through credit, prices in orthodox pre-war fashion); and so long as this is the case, gold must continue to flow there. The stream can be stopped (so long as a change in the gold value of the dollar is ruled out of the question) only in one of two ways—either by a fall in the value of the dollar or by an increase in the value of gold in the outside world. The former of these alternatives, namely the depreciation of the dollar through inflation in the United States, is that on which many English authorities have based their hopes. But it could only come about by a reversal or defeat of the present policy of the Federal Reserve Board. Moreover, the volume of redundant gold is now so great, and the capacity of the rest of the world for its absorption so much reduced, that the inflation would need to be prolonged and determined to produce the required result. Dollar prices would have to rise very high before America's impoverished customers, starving for real goods and having no use for barren metal, would relieve her of £200 million worth of gold in preference to taking commodities. The banking authorities of the United States would be likely to notice in good time that, if the gold is not wanted and must be got rid of, it would be much simpler just to reduce the dollar price of gold. The only way of selling redundant stocks of anything, whether gold or copper or wheat, is to abate the price.

The alternative method, namely the increase in the value of gold in the outside world, could scarcely be brought about unless some other country or countries stepped in to relieve the United States of the duty of burying unwanted gold. Great Britain, France, Italy, Holland, Sweden, Argentina, Japan, and many other countries have fully as much unoccupied gold as they require for an emergency store. Nor is there anything to prevent them from buying gold now if they prefer gold to other things.

The notion, that America can get rid of her gold by showing a greater readiness to make loans to foreign countries, is incomplete. This result will only follow if the loans are inflationary loans, not provided for by the reduction of expenditure and investment in other directions. Foreign investments formed out of real savings will no more denude the United States of her gold than they denude Great Britain of hers. But if the United States places a large amount of dollar purchasing power in the hands of foreigners, as a pure addition to the purchasing power previously in the hands of her own nationals, then no doubt prices will rise and we shall be back on the method of depreciating the dollar, just discussed, by a normal inflationary process. Thus the invitation to the United States to deal with the problem of her gold by increasing her foreign investments will not be effective unless it is intended as an invitation to inflate.

I argue, therefore, that the same policy which is wise for Great Britain is wise for the United States, namely to aim at the stability of the commodity value of the dollar rather than at stability of the gold value of the dollar, and to effect the former if necessary by varying the gold value of the dollar.

If Great Britain and the United States were both embarked on this policy and if both were successful, our secondary desideratum, namely the stability of the dollar-exchange standard, would follow as a consequence. I agree with Mr Hawtrey that the ideal state of affairs is an intimate co-operation between the Federal Reserve Board and the Bank of England, as a result of which stability of prices and of exchange would be achieved at the same time. But I suggest that it is wiser and more practical that this should be allowed to develop out of experience and mutual advantage, without either side binding itself to the other. If the Bank of England aims primarily at the stability of sterling, and the Federal Reserve Board at the stability of dollars, each authority letting the other into its confidence so far as may be, better results will be obtained than if sterling is unalterably fixed by law in terms of dollars and the Bank of England is limited to using its influence on the Federal Reserve Board to keep dollars steady. A collaboration which is not free on both sides is likely to lead to dissensions, especially if the business of keeping dollars steady involves a heavy expenditure in burying unwanted gold.

We have reached a stage in the evolution of money when a 'managed' currency is inevitable, but we have not yet reached the point when the management can be entrusted to a single authority. The best we can do, therefore, is to have *two* managed currencies, sterling and dollars, with as close a collaboration as possible between the aims and methods of the managements.

3. *Other countries*

What course, in such an event, should other countries pursue? It is necessary to presume to begin with that we are dealing with countries which have not lost control of their currencies. But a stage can and should be reached before long at which nearly all countries have regained the control. In Russia, Poland, and Germany it is only necessary that the governments should develop some other source of revenue than the inflationary or turnover tax on the use of money discussed in chapter 2. In France and Italy it is only necessary that the franc and the lira should be devaluated at a level at which the service of the internal debt is within the capacity of the taxpayer.

Control having been regained, there are probably no countries, other than Great Britain and the United States, which would be justified in attempting to set up an independent standard. Their wisest course would be to base their currencies either on sterling or on dollars by means of an exchange standard, fixing their exchanges in terms of one or the other (though preserving, perhaps, a discretion to vary in the event of a serious divergence between sterling and dollars), and maintaining stability by holding reserves of gold at home and balances in London and New York to meet short-period fluctuations, and by using bank rate and other methods to regulate the volume of purchasing power, and thus to maintain stability of relative price level, over longer periods.

Perhaps the British Empire (apart from Canada) and the countries of Europe would adopt the sterling standard; whilst Canada and the other countries of North and South America would adopt the dollar standard. But each could choose freely, until, with the progress of knowledge and understanding, so perfect a harmony had been established between the two that the choice was a matter of indifference.

Appendix I

When it diverged greatly from the text on page 42 above, the original article 'Inflation as a Method of Taxation' concluded as follows:

This is another way of putting what economists mean by the velocity of circulation increasing when a currency loses credit. The public try to protect themselves in this way when they have been convinced by experience that their money is always falling in value and that every holder of it loses.

These theoretical considerations are of the utmost practical importance at the present time, because several currencies have now entered on this second phase. In the last stages of inflation the prodigious increase in the velocity of circulation may have more effect in raising prices and depreciating the exchanges than the increase in the volume of notes; and the note-issuing authorities cry out against what they regard as the unfair phenomenon of the value of the notes falling *more* than in proportion to their increased volume.

In Moscow the unwillingness to hold money except for the shortest possible time reaches a fantastic intensity. If you buy a pound of cheese in a grocer's shop, the grocer runs off with the roubles as fast as his legs will carry him to the Central Market to replenish his stocks by changing them into cheese again, lest they lose their value before he gets there. This is what keeps the new bourgeoisie so thin, and justifies the prevision of economists in naming the phenomenon 'velocity of circulation'. In Vienna mushroom exchange banks have sprung up at every street corner, where you can change your krone into Zurich francs within a few minutes of receiving them, and so avoid the risk of loss during the time it will take you to reach your usual bank. A prudent man at a café ordering a bock of beer will order a second bock at the same time, at the expense of drinking it tepid, lest the price rise meanwhile.

The tendency of the notes, in the latter stages of the *degringolade*, to fall in value at a greater rate than the inflation is sometimes regarded as an anomalous and temporary phenomenon. It is nothing of the kind; it is merely the only method left open to the public to evade a crushing burden.

The argument may be illustrated by figures. The following table shows the gold value of the German note issue at various dates:

	Volume of note issue in milliard paper marks	Number of paper marks = 1 gold mark	Value of note issue in milliard gold marks
December 1920	81	17	4·8
December 1921	122	46	2·7
March 1922	140	65	2·2
June 1922	178	90	1·9

Thus, while the note issue has been a little more than doubled in the period covered by these figures, the value of the note has fallen to less than a fifth; that is to say, the depreciation has proceeded more than twice as fast as the inflation. Instead of having to issue twice as many notes to provide a given sum in gold the German government has to issue more than five times as many.

The corresponding figures for Austria are as follows:

	Volume of note issue in milliard paper krone	Number of paper krone = 1 gold krone	Value of note issue in million gold krone
December 1920	30	60	500
December 1921	174	500	348
April 1922	347	1,500	231
June 1922	470	3,450	136

Austria being at a more advanced phase of taxing by inflation, these figures exhibit the same phenomenon in a more marked degree. Whereas eighteen months ago the gold value of the note issue was more than £20 million, the present value is less than £6 million; and no one can say how many milliard notes the Austrian government would now have to print in order to raise £6 million, real resources.

On the other hand, both in Germany and Austria a diminution in the velocity of circulation, brought about by a renewal of confidence, might lead to a very great recovery in the value of marks and krone, quite irrespective of any diminution in the volume of circulation. Thus, if it were believed that the process of inflation had come to an end, the notes would greatly increase in value without any actual deflation being necessary.

The figures for Russia show the same phenomenon more markedly still:

	Notes outstanding in milliard paper roubles	Number of paper roubles = 1 gold rouble	Value of note issue in million gold roubles
January 1919	61	103	592
January 1920	225	1,670	134
January 1921	1,169	26,000	45
January 1922	17,539	172,000	102[1]
March 1922	48,535	1,060,000	46
May 1922	145,635	3,800,000	38

[1] The anomalous figure for January 1922, as compared with the previous January, is due to the reintroduction of the use of money in State transactions as a result of the new economic policy.

Thus in Russia we have the last phase. Clearly a note issue worth less than £4 million cannot be adequate for the transaction of the business of

Russia even in its present condition. A point has been reached when, to a large extent, the of money is dispensed with altogether. It is improbable that the Soviet government could raise another £5 million real resources by this method, however many notes they might print.

Nevertheless, this instrument of taxation has been extremely effective in the past. The Soviet government themselves calculate that the purchasing power secured to the State by printing notes has amounted to the following sums:

	million gold roubles
1918	525
1919	380
1920	186
1921	143
1922 (January to (March)	58

or (say) £130 million altogether

It is common to speak as though, when a government pays its way by inflation, the people of the country avoid taxation. This is not so. What the German government raises by printing notes is just as much taken from the German people (except in so far as foreigners can be induced to buy and hoard the notes) as though it had been taken by more orthodox means. I should estimate very roughly that for some time past the German government has been obtaining from this source something between £75 million and £100 million per annum (of which, however, a useful proportion has been contributed by speculative foreigners). The difficulties of the German government at the present time are as much due to the tendency of this source of revenue to dry up as to the current demands for cash on reparation account, though it is the weight of these demands which is finally breaking the system. Germany is just reaching the phase, already reached by Austria and Russia, when the real yield of note-printing begins to diminish at a great pace.

The same arguments which I have here applied to the note issue can be extended, with a few modifications, to all the forms of internal government debt. The indirect results of this form of finance I discuss in detail in the third section of this Supplement [i.e. in Chapter 1 above (Ed.)].

What a government spends the public pay for. There is no such thing as an uncovered deficit. But in some countries, apparently, it is possible to please and content the public, for a time at least, by giving them, in return for the taxes they pay, finely engraved receipts on water-marked paper. The income tax receipts, which we in England receive from the Surveyor, we throw into the wastepaper basket; in Germany they call them banknotes and put them into their pocket-books; in France they are termed *rentes* and are locked up in the family safe.

Appendix II

When it diverged greatly from the text on page 80 above, the original article 'The Theory of the Exchanges and "Purchasing Power Parity"' concluded as follows:

Thus a tendency of these two measures of the value of a country's currency to move differently is a highly interesting symptom; but it is not possible to say, without a further examination of each special case, of what exactly it is significant. Let me illustrate these theories by a brief examination of the actual figures charted below.

The first of these charts,[1] which deals with the value of sterling, illustrates the significance of the choice of a base period. The top line, which gives the purchasing power parity calculated with 1913 as base, remains steadily above the actual exchange, but the second line, which is the same thing calculated with August 1919 as base, displays a persevering tendency to come together with the actual exchange, the line of which it is very frequently crossing. If we could depend on an inductive argument, it would be tempting to conclude from this chart that the events of the war have depressed the equilibrium of the purchasing power parity of sterling as against the dollar by about 6 per cent, but that with this adjustment the theory has worked very well indeed for the past two and a half years.

This chart also brings out rather clearly the susceptibility of the foreign exchange rates to seasonal influences, whereas the purchasing power parity is decidedly less affected by them. In each year the biggest divergencies are seen in the autumn, except that in 1921 the movement came unduly early—that is to say, in July, the exchange market having anticipated the usual autumnal excess of exports from the United States, which, in face of the depression of trade, failed to materialise on the usual scale, as is very clearly brought out by the chart attached to Mr Falk's article below.[2] The large part played by seasonal influences in the case of the sterling exchange, where progressive deterioration due to currency inflation is no longer present, corroborates the opinion expressed in my article, given above, on stabilising the exchanges, that a great deal can be performed of high value to commerce by an attempt to minimise the seasonal movement by means of an adequately supported gold standard.

[1] The charts for France and Italy appear in the book (page 87) and are not reproduced here. Those for England, Sweden and Germany appear below [Ed.].
[2] O. T. Falk, 'The Dollar–European Exchanges: The Bearing of Seasonal Fluctuations', *Manchester Guardian Commercial, Reconstruction in Europe*, 20 April 1922, page 22.

The curves for Sweden are not only unique amongst European countries in that the exchange is above, instead of below, the purchasing power parity, but are also anomalous in other respects, partly as a result of its geographical situation towards Russia and Germany and its use as a depository for the foreign balances of these countries, especially Russia. But in this case there seems to have been a tendency in recent months for the pre-war equilibrium to be re-established.

In the case of France the curves are coming together again after abnormal

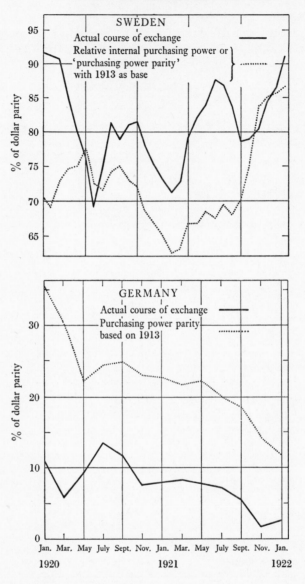

divergencies during 1920; but this has been brought about as much by a fall in the internal purchasing power of the franc as by any recovery in the mean rate of exchange.

For Italy, rather unexpectedly perhaps, the theory seems to have held very well, although here, as in the case of France and Great Britain, there are indications that the war has resulted in a permanent lowering of the equilibrium point, for the concordance would be decidedly closer if the curves were recharted with August, 1919, as the base date. The Italian curve illustrates in a remarkable way the manner in which the external and internal purchasing powers of the currency fall together, where the main influence at work is a progressive depreciation due to inflation.

The curve for Germany (which is calculated on a slightly different principle) is in one respect a little misleading to the eye, for it may appear that the divergence between the two curves has remained fairly steady, with a certain tendency to diminish. This is because, with so huge an absolute fall, equal *percentage* changes appear as smaller and smaller *absolute* changes. For example, external purchasing power in January 1922 was only 20 per cent of its value in July 1920, whereas internal purchasing power at the latter date was still nearly 50 per cent what it had been at the earlier date. If the index number taken had been one of general purchasing power instead of working-class cost of living the discrepancy would not have been quite so great. Nevertheless it is clear that, as a result of the recent exchange slump, the external purchasing power of the mark has been falling much faster than its internal purchasing power, so much so that, even allowing for the persisting consequences of reparation payments, it is most unlikely that the present position can be one of equilibrium. Hence, if the exchange value of the mark does not improve we must expect internal prices in Germany to rise sharply—perhaps to double what they were in January of this year (quite apart from upward changes elsewhere), an influence charged with social and political consequences which cannot be calculated. If, on the other hand, the German budget were to be balanced and the issue of new currency were to be checked from now onwards (which, however, in the present situation of reparations, is impossible), then the present excessive divergence between the two curves would tend, as time went on, to be partly cured by an improvement in the exchanges.

In the table below the *Economist* index number has been taken for England, the index of the 'Statistique Générale' for France, 'Ricardo Bachi' for Italy, and the *Svensk Handelstidning* for Sweden. These index numbers, reduced (where necessary) to percentages of the 1913 price level, are taken as a measure of the purchasing power of money in the four countries concerned, and are then expressed in terms of a percentage of the purchasing power of money in the United States, as measured by the Bureau of Labour index. The values so obtained are then compared with the exchange values of the four different currencies in the foreign exchange markets, averaged monthly, and expressed as percentages of dollar parity.

The following purchasing power parity table and chart for German marks

PURCHASING POWER PARITY

	Index numbers % of 1913 average					Purchasing power % of 1913 purchasing power (viz. reciprocals of column 1)					Purchasing power % of dollar purchasing power					Actual monthly average value of exchange % of $ par			
											Eng.								
											Based on 1913	Based on Aug. 1919	Fr.	It.	Sw.	Eng.	Fr.	It.	Sw.
	Eng.	Fr.	It.	Sw.	U.S.A.	Eng.	Fr.	It.	Sw.	U.S.A.									
1919																			
August	242	349	369	321	226	41·3	28·6	27·1	31·1	44·2	93·4	87·6	64·7	61·3	70·4	87·6	66·0	56·2	91·7
September	245	362	372	319	220	40·9	27·6	26·9	31·3	45·4	90·1	84·5	60·8	59·2	69·0	85·8	61·3	53·0	91·3
October	252	384	391	307	223	39·6	26·0	25·6	32·6	44·8	88·4	82·9	58·0	57·1	72·8	85·9	60·3	51·1	90·3
November	259	407	439	308	230	38·5	24·6	22·8	32·5	43·5	88·5	83·0	56·5	52·4	74·7	84·3	55·2	44·2	86·0
December	273	425	457	317	238	36·6	23·5	21·9	31·5	42·0	87·1	81·7	55·9	52·1	75·0	78·4	48·3	39·9	80·8
1920																			
January	289	489	504	319	248	34·7	20·4	19·8	31·3	40·3	86·1	80·9	50·5	49·1	77·7	75·6	44·4	37·2	77·2
February	303	525	556	342	249	33·0	19·1	18·0	29·2	40·2	82·1	77·0	47·5	44·8	72·6	69·5	36·5	28·6	69·4
March	310	557	619	354	253	32·2	17·9	16·1	28·2	39·5	81·5	76·4	45·3	40·7	71·4	76·2	37·1	27·6	75·7
April	306	591	679	361	265	32·7	16·9	14·7	27·7	37·7	86·7	81·3	44·8	39·0	74·3	80·6	32·1	22·9	81·4
May	305	553	659	366	272	32·8	18·1	15·2	27·3	36·8	89·1	83·6	49·2	41·3	75·3	81·1	41·0	26·6	78·9
June	291	495	614	363	269	34·3	20·2	16·3	27·5	37·2	92·2	86·5	54·3	43·8	73·4	81·1	42·3	30·6	81·4
July	293	498	613	363	262	34·3	20·1	16·3	27·5	38·2	89·5	83·9	52·6	42·7	72·0	79·4	42·3	30·0	81·5
August	288	504	631	365	250	34·7	19·8	15·8	27·4	40·0	86·7	83·3	49·5	39·5	68·5	74·2	37·5	25·1	76·5
September	284	528	661	362	242	35·2	18·9	15·1	27·6	41·3	85·2	79·9	45·8	36·6	66·8	72·2	34·9	22·6	75·3
October	266	502	662	346	225	37·5	19·9	15·1	28·9	44·4	84·4	79·2	44·0	34·0	65·0	71·4	33·9	20·2	73·5
November	246	460	658	331	207	40·7	21·7	15·2	30·2	48·3	84·2	79·0	44·9	31·5	62·5	70·7	31·2	18·7	71·2
December	220	434	635	299	189	45·5	23·0	15·7	33·4	52·9	85·0	80·7	43·5	29·7	63·1	71·4	30·7	18·1	73·0
1921																			
January	209	407	642	267	178	47·9	24·6	15·6	37·5	56·2	85·3	80·0	43·8	27·7	66·7	76·7	33·3	18·4	79·5
February	192	377	613	250	167	52·0	26·5	16·3	40·0	59·9	86·8	81·4	44·3	27·2	66·8	79·6	37·2	18·9	82·9
March	189	360	604	237	162	52·8	27·8	16·6	42·2	61·7	85·5	80·2	45·0	26·9	68·4	80·3	36·5	19·8	84·9
April	183	347	584	229	154	54·6	28·8	17·1	43·7	64·9	84·1	79·8	44·4	26·3	67·3	80·7	37·1	23·8	87·8
May	182	329	547	218	151	54·9	30·4	18·3	45·9	66·2	82·9	77·7	45·9	27·6	69·3	81·5	43·3	26·7	86·8
June	179	325	509	218	148	56·0	30·8	19·6	45·9	67·6	82·9	77·7	45·6	29·0	67·9	78·0	41·9	25·8	83·6
July	178	330	520	211	148	56·1	30·3	19·2	47·4	67·6	83·0	77·8	44·8	28·4	70·2	74·8	40·5	23·6	78·7
August	179	332	542	198	152	55·9	30·0	18·5	50·5	65·8	85·0	79·7	45·6	28·1	76·8	75·1	40·2	22·3	79·1
September	183	345	580	182	152	54·7	29·0	17·2	50·5	65·8	83·2	78·0	43·1	26·2	83·6	76·5	37·9	22·0	80·9
October	170	332	599	175	150	58·7	30·1	16·7	57·1	66·7	88·0	82·5	45·1	25·1	85·6	79·5	37·9	20·5	85·3
November	166	332	595	174	149	60·4	30·1	16·8	57·5	67·1	90·0	84·4	44·9	25·0	85·7	81·5	37·4	21·4	86·5
December	162	326	595	172	149	61·8	30·7	16·8	58·1	67·1	92·0	86·3	45·7	25·0	86·6	85·3	40·5	23·0	91·3

Eng., England; Fr., France; It., Italy; Sw., Sweden.

are based on information contained in articles contributed by Moritz Elsas to the *Economic Journal* for September 1921 (p. 331), and March 1922 (p. 69). In this case the figures for internal and external purchasing power are calculated with reference to the 'cost of living' (not a general index of wholesale commodity prices); and are based on England (*Labour Gazette*), not on the United States:

	Cost of living index (Elsas) pre-war 26·5	Purchasing power per cent of 1913	Purchasing power per cent of sterling purchasing power	Actual course of exchange per cent of sterling parity
1920				
January	170	15·6	35·1	10·9
March	198	13·4	30·8	6·0
May	289	9·2	22·2	9·3
July	277	9·6	24·2	13·5
September	281	9·4	24·5	11·6
November	316	8·4	23·2	7·6
1921				
January	311	8·5	22·5	7·8
March	297	8·9	21·4	8·5
May	280	9·5	21·6	7·8
July	293	9·0	19·7	7·3
September	319	8·3	18·3	5·1
November	382	6·9	14·0	1·9
1922				
January	439	6·0	11·5	2·6

Appendix III

PRINTING ERRORS IN THE FIRST EDITION CORRECTED IN THE PRESENT EDITION

Reference in the Present Edition		Reference in the First Edition		Correction
page	*line*	*page*	*line*	
20				
footnote 2	7			
and		22		
footnote 3	2–3	footnote 1	2	For 'high' read 'low'
81	4	98	11	For 'Europe' read 'Westropa'
82		100		
footnote 1	3	footnote 1	4	For 'index' read 'exchange'
111	22	134	23	Insert 'it' before 'is' to follow the article
142	25	179	20	For 'Reserve' read 'Account'
143	7	180	5	For 'Reserve' read 'Account'
143	28	181	2	For 'Reserve' read 'Account'
144	1	181	10	For 'Reserve' read 'Account'
144	18	182	4	For 'Reserve' read 'Account'
152	31	194	18	For 'three months before' read 'the same month as'

INDEX

American debt, 150
Aurelian, 124, 125
Austria, elasticity of demand for money, 43
  value of note issue, 45
  currency of, 48

Bank of England, and forward exchange, 112
  and gold, 137, 149, 152, 153
  and existing system, 142
Bank rate, and prices, 20
  and forward exchange, 112
  pre-war effect of, 129
'Big Five', 142
British Empire, currency of, 160
Business class, 17-25

Cannan, Professor, 42
Capital, diminution of, 28
Capital levy, *versus* currency depreciation,
  53, 55
  in Great Britain, 57
Cassel, Professor, 71, 75n
Chervonetz, 45, 46, 49 and n
Consols, 11-12, 14, 15
Credit cycle, 67, 68, 148
Cunliffe Committee, 116, 145, 152, 153
Cuno, Dr, 50, 51n
Currency depreciation, in history, 8-10
  advantage to debtor class, 9
  incidence of, 37
  versus capital levy, 53
  social evils of, 55
Czechoslovakia, 118, 120

Debtor class, political influence of, 10
Deflation, 117
  and distribution of wealth, 3
  and production of wealth, 3, 29
  meaning of, 67
  arguments for, 121-4
  and Aurelian, 125
Devaluation, 53, 54
  and deflation, 116, 117
  and currency reform, 119
Dollar, forward exchange in, 96-8, 101, 102

Edward III, 131
Equation of exchange, 76, 80, 81

Estcourt, Dr, 88n
Exchange speculation, effect of, 92
  and forward market, 109, 114
  services of, 112-13
External purchasing power, 71

Federal Reserve Board, and gold, 69n, 134,
  139, 154-5
  index number, 76
  co-operation with, 147
Fisher, Professor Irving, 63n, 122, 126, 131,
  147-8
Foreign exchange, and purchasing power
  parity, 71-2
  forward market in, 94
  stability of, 116, 126, 147
Forward market in exchanges, 94
  as an insurance, 102
  and interest rates, 104
  and state banks, 110
  and bank rate, 112
Franc, exchange, 60
  purchasing power parity, 83, 85
  seasonal movement, 91
  forward exchange in, 96, 97, 98, 103, 104
  devaluation of, 118, 123
France, losses of investors, 12, 59
  burden of internal debts, 58

Genoa Conference, 110, 112, 117, 118n, 138
Germany, interest rates in, 22
  and currency inflation, 36
  elasticity of demand for money in, 43
  value of note issue, 45
  currency of, 47
  sums raised by inflation, 51
  recent financial history, 52
  equation of exchange, 82
Gibbon, 124
Gold and state banks, 65-6
  price of, 150
  cost of burying, 156
Gold discoveries, 132
Gold-mining, 133
Gold standard, 8, 10-11
  restoration of, 123, 132
Great Britain, capital levy in, 57
  currency statistics of, 67

171